MW01075721

Spirto
Gentil

Spirto Gentil

An Invitation to Listen to Great Music
with LUIGI GIUSSANI

Revised and Edited by
Maurizio Maniscalco
and **Gregory Wolfe**

Foreword by
Sir Stephen Hough

SL/.NT
B O O K S

SPIRTO GENTIL
An Invitation to Listen to Great Music with Luigi Giussani

Copyright © 2025 Fraternità di comunione e liberazione. All rights reserved. Except for brief quotations in critical publications or reviews, no part of this book may be reproduced in any manner without prior written permission from the publisher. Write: Permissions, Slant Books, P.O. Box 60295, Seattle, WA 98160.

Slant Books
P.O. Box 60295
Seattle, WA 98160

www.slantbooks.org

Cataloguing-in-Publication data:

Names: Giussani, Luigi.

Title: Spirto Gentil: An invitation to listen to great music with Luigi Giussani / Luigi Giussani.

Description: Seattle, WA: Slant Books, 2025

Identifiers: ISBN 978-1-63982-188-4 (hardcover) | ISBN 978-1-63982-187-7 (paperback) | ISBN 978-1-63982-189-1 (ebook)

Subjects: LCSH: Music | Music History | Music History and criticism | Music appreciation

Contents

PART II: MOMENTS IN THE HISTORY OF THE CHURCH

PART III: A PEOPLE SINGS

IL DIRETTORE MUSICALE

Milano, 15 ottobre 2002

Caro Monsignor Giussani,

vorrei partecipare alla festa dei Suoi ottant'anni con i miei auguri.

E dicendoLe semplicemente "grazie" per quello che Lei ha dato alla musica, indicandola a tanti giovani come l'esperienza che più ci comunica il mistero. Come strada per la ricerca della felicità.

E' un mistero che non ha bisogno di parole, ci afferra più in fondo. Da dove arriva?

In me resta questa domanda e Gliel'affido mentre con Lei voglio condividere questi versi di Dante, nel Canto XIV del Paradiso, che hanno segnato la mia vita.

"E come giga e arpa, in tempra tesa
di molte corde, fa dolce tintinno
a tal da cui la nota non è intesa,

così da' lumi che lì m'apparinno
s'accogliea per la croce una melode
che mi rapiva, senza intender l'inno."

Con affetto, Suo

Riccardo Muti

20121 Milano - Via Filodrammatici, 2 - Tel. +39.02.8879.1 - Fax +39.02.7200.3820

Dear Monsignor Giussani,

I would like to participate in the celebration of your eighty years with my best wishes.

And to tell you simply "thank you" for what you have given to music, indicating it to so many young people as the experience that best communicates the mystery. As a path for the search for happiness.

It is a mystery that does not need words, that grasps us deep down. Where does it come from?

This question remains in me, and I entrust it to you while I want to share with you these verses from Dante in Canto XIV of the *Paradiso*, which have marked my life.

*And just as harp and viol, whose many chords
are tempered, taut, produce sweet harmony
although each single note is not distinct,*

*so, from the light that then appeared to me,
out from that cross there spread a melody
that held me rapt, although I could not tell*

what hymn it was.

With affection,
Yours,
Riccardo Muti

FOREWORD

"MUSIC IS MY RELIGION." It is quite common to hear this from music lovers, reluctant to admit they believe in nothing because music is so obviously *something*, and its intangible vibrations in the air resonate so deep in the human heart. Concerts become this agnostic's liturgy and visits to summer festivals a kind of yearly retreat. Instead of undermining this attitude it is possible to see Fr. Giussani's tiny essays as a starting point in a discussion, because music connects us with beauty which, whether we realize it or not, can be a bridge between human and divine life. To be overcome by Beethoven's String Quartet op. 132, to use one of the author's examples, is to find oneself in a state of prayer, of gratitude, of recognition: "[T]his music becomes our voice in the personal and intimate dialogue with him and at the same time the perception of his reply."

The author as adolescent remembers the "instant and the thrill" when music opened the door to God's existence. A human voice singing on a recording; an intimation that this didn't so much prove the existence of God as *enact* his existence in that moment. It was an Emmaus encounter, a recognition that Something *was*. And that existence was not so much a presence as a present: a gift of happiness, the desire for which is the alpha and omega of human existence itself.

There is an infectious charm in the openness and, dare I say, naïveté with which Giussani shares his thoughts with us. As we read these reflections we are led into a sense of wonder at the sheer beauty of music, at its ability to express things which are beyond words, to amplify our joy, to empathize with our sorrow and pain, to sing with mercy and with love. Music cannot be a religion in itself: indeed, it has been the background to some of the greatest evils in human history; but it reflects and expresses who we are in our thirst to be satisfied and fulfilled. "For I wish it so! What I wish I still don't know," as Marc Blitzstein's song so poignantly puts it.

One of Giussani's key insights as a theologian is Christianity as an encounter with Jesus which becomes an event. Doesn't this sound like a concert experience? To take a seat and come face to face with the presence of music's ordered sound-waves, to meet them with attention so that the experience becomes an event. Never mind a renewal of the Christian experience, there is a template here for a renewal of the concert experience.

Giussani spoke of the spiritual life as "the development of a gaze." This also struck me because it encapsulates why classical music in its demand for concentration is different from other music—different, I hasten to add, not better. Unlike literature or painting, music takes place in time. To stand in front of a canvas or to turn the pages of a novel is determined by the viewer or reader, whether a couple of distracted seconds or a couple of concentrated hours. In music, sounds pass by in an unstoppable flow. We need to travel with them or we miss them. The challenge for a performer is to bring the audience along with us. To keep the "gaze" in focus.

"Let's go together." I can't think of a better invitation from a musician to an audience than these words of Fr. Giussani. We initiate a journey when we perform but we do not travel alone. And isn't that God's own invitation to humanity in Christ?

—Sir Stephen Hough

What You Are Looking For Exists

Bellini, Donizetti, Puccini, Rossini, Verdi
Spirto Gentil: Opera Pieces

I STILL REMEMBER the instant and the thrill—the yearning of the instant—when the fact of God's existence became evident, filled with meaning for my life.

I was in seminary, in the third year of high school. During our singing lessons, for the first quarter of an hour, the professor would usually illustrate the history of music by having us listen to records. That day, a 78 rpm record started going round on the turntable and the song of a tenor who at the time was very famous suddenly broke the silence of the classroom. With a powerful voice full of vibrations, Tito Schipa began an aria from the fourth act of Donizetti's *La Favorita*: *Spirto gentil, ne' sogni miei, brillasti un dì, ma ti perdei. Fuggi dal cor mentita speme, larve d'amor fuggite insieme* ["Gentle spirit, you once shone in my dreams, but after, I lost you forever: leave my frail heart, you false promises, you ghosts of love"]. *Spirto gentil, ne' sogni miei*: when the very first note vibrated on the air, I intuited, heartrendingly, that what is called "God"—by which I mean the inevitable destiny for which a person is born—is the ultimate end of the need for happiness, the happiness that the heart irrepressibly needs.

As soon as I heard *Spirto gentil*, in that precise instant of my life, I understood for the first time that God existed, and thus that nothing could exist without a meaning; that the heart could not exist unless the heart's goal existed: happiness.

Man's heart—the human I—is the need for happiness; this is Christianity's first word. If we do not start with this, we cannot understand any of the rest. In that third year of high school, in the timbre of that voice, I had perceived the thrill of something that was missing, not from the beautiful song of Donizetti's romance, but from my life: there was something missing and it would not find support, fulfillment, an answer, satisfaction, anywhere. And yet the heart demands an answer; it lives only for this.

Man's dignity is indicated by the word "happiness": *Spirto gentil, ne' sogni miei, brillasti un dì, ma ti perdei. Fuggi dal cor mentita speme larve d'amor fuggite insieme.* Can anything be experienced more intensely than uttering seriously the word "happiness"?

I cannot say that in that music class in the third year of high school I understood exhaustively the core of the question, but I had a foretaste of it: just like when you have a seed in your hand and you foresee that it can grow to become a tall tree.

I would understand what that thrill meant only slowly, with the passing years, after having the surprise of it almost daily. For only time makes you understand what the seed is and what it has inside it. The first time you see the seed, you cannot understand what it contains; only if you have already seen how it develops can you understand what a seed is. This is what that first thrilling instant was for me, when I perceived the ultimate yearning that defines the heart of man when he is not distracted by vanities that burn up in just a few seconds. It was all still only a shadowy outline; but when, the following year, my excellent philosophy teacher read us Leopardi's hymn "To His Lady," I felt a sudden sense of corroboration that enlarged—as well as confirmed in me—the impression I had received from listening to Donizetti's *La Favorita*.

The subsequent development of my religious consciousness was totally influenced by that experience I had in the third year of high school. This first impact communicated an inevitable thrill that made my subject—that is, my "I," my person—real in that instant as a thirst for happiness, even with an uncertain response; or rather, with a response incapable of sustaining itself, that is, if it relied only on the flesh. And yet it is precisely in the flesh—that is to say, within reality—that the answer comes. The fact of Christ—the existence of God in the flesh—depicts the face of this emergence of the divine in history. From that moment, for the eye and the heart of the man who encounters that Fact, this certainty can never again be lacking.

Seen in this light, everything for me is colored by the analogy with the immediate and great relationship I had with my father and mother. My father, at a certain point and thereafter—when I was already in seminary—when I would return home for vacation, before going to bed, my father would always repeat to me: "Find a reason for everything." I would wish him a good night, and he would say to me: "Find a reason for everything, pay attention to the reasons for everything." The figure of my father dominates my life. For example, when he would solve in two minutes all the problems at home—those immediate problems that make a husband angry with his wife, parents with their children, children with their parents—by singing a line from opera: *La donna è mobile qual piuma al vento* ["woman is as changeable as a feather in the wind"]. He would sing and everything would fall into place, not by magic, but by virtue. Because it was planned, it was willed. For this reason, too, I owe a debt of gratitude to the greats of opera.

PART I

The Great Masters

A "Fount of Mercy" That Makes Man New

Wolfgang Amadeus Mozart
Requiem

Anna Tomowa-Sintow, Helga Müller Molinari, Vinson Cole,
Paata Burchuladze, Vienna Singverein
Vienna Philharmonic directed by Herbert Von Karajan

MOZART, A SUPREME artist and a profoundly Christian one, presents in his *Requiem* humanity's evil, the world's hate, and sin's malice within the reverberation of God's mercy.

On one hand, he leads us with his music into the tremendous choice of the man who refuses God. The word that best expresses this refusal is *forgetting*; this is an experience that adults have. A child is inattentive but an adult cannot be inattentive. Therefore, forgetting is, in essence, a refusal. So forgetting is a refusal. Can there be a greater injustice or crime? Imagine a baby still in his mother's womb but capable of thinking, that is, already aware; imagine that he refuses his mother, denies, forgets his mother, who in every instant is part of his being through the food and life that she communicates to him. The world's injustice is forgetfulness of God; the injustice in your life and my life is forgetfulness of God; this is the "crime" from which all other crimes derive.

We can identify the source of the refusal and thus the source of evil—evil in the world, which becomes our evil. Everyone would accept Jesus as long as he remained the ancient symbol of the Child Jesus, fountain of tenderness and kindness, the evocation of good, the symbol of moral value. When does the refusal begin? When, Péguy would say, "his mission begins." Christ's mission is not the call to moral values, but rather his claim to be the savior of the world, the savior of my life. If this is true, he alone becomes the source of the characteristics that my life and the society must have: my life and the life of society must depend on him. This is intolerable for the world and thus intolerable, despite our reticence, for us. Man claims to know what is right for life; if he does not get what he wants and in the way he wants it, he rebels. It cannot be denied that this is an injustice—this is injustice itself.

And yet, in the *Requiem* we are faced with a paradox: at the same time, in the same phrase it says: "King of awesome majesty . . . grant your forgiveness, merciful Lord Jesus, grant them your rest." Thus, the terrible and the merciful, justice and grace, exist side by side. And even more paradoxically, mercy will overcome the evil of injustice. Mercy is greater than condemnation: it overflows the boundaries of condemnation. For this reason, pardon or mercy constitute a decisive factor in the definition of sin, speaking in Christian terms, because when they enter into sin they change it. This is not the exaltation of the Protestant attitude in which Christ does everything without humanity: it is the sinner who cries out, it is the sinner who in his sin prays, in his sin can already pray. The space between our forgetting and our redemption is overcome.

Every phrase of the *Requiem* (as the music makes evident) begins with the undisputed affirmation of the dominion of justice and truth—and then it is as though we are suddenly interrupted by something that comes in and unexpectedly sweetens the harshness of justice, the acrid affirmation of truth, softening it into a plea, a supplication, that somehow knows it can be made. *Rex tremendae majestatis*: king of terrible majesty, whom no man can touch (the tower of Babel is the emblem of the collective effort of all humankind to dethrone God, to conceive a world without God). But then, suddenly, *Qui salvandos salvas gratis*: you who desire salvation, you who are gracious and loving, *Salvame, fons pietatis*, save my life, fountain of love.

As Péguy teaches us, "What defines our disaster is that our miseries themselves are no longer Christian." The great question is the fact that man is originally wounded. That our miseries be Christian means, basically, that our miseries are aware of themselves as being initially caused by original sin, by this mortal wound. We are born with a mortal wound, like a child who cannot survive and is about to die. That "our miseries themselves are no longer Christian" means first of all our forgetfulness, the obliteration, the total censorship in life and culture—in my life, in the life of each of us—of original sin, of the fact that we are born with a rupture, a wound, a mortal flaw. Wound or mortal flaw means that we cannot be ourselves: we are born without the ability to be ourselves. And yet there can be no true act of our conscious life if it does not arise from our awareness of being sinners.

In this "un-Christian," de-Christianized world, man has no hope of pardon; he does not know what pardon means, he does not know what it means to be forgiven, and thus he cannot remake himself, he cannot make himself anew because to be made new he has to feel himself forgiven. Christian misery is the misery that feels itself invaded, surrounded, and embraced by forgiveness, like a child in the arms of its mother. *Rex . . . qui salvandos salvas gratis, salva me fons pietatis*: this is what man needed, this is what man needs, what I need today, now: a *fons pietatis*, a fountain of mercy. Because then I am remade, I begin to be myself.

"But," Péguy goes on, "Jesus came. He didn't pass his years on earth whining and questioning the evil of the times. He went right to the point. In a very simple way. By creating Christianity." Jesus came—the fount, the source of mercy, the *fons pietatis*—came. The fount of mercy comes—it comes now, like a mother who sees and embraces her child. You may have forgotten it until now, you may have not known it until now: now it is here. Jesus comes, and without wasting time what does he do? He does not reject the damned, he does not calculate or judge, he does not anticipate the Judgment Day in order to avoid its eternal bitterness: he creates Christianity. What does Christianity mean? Christianity is the tie that Christ establishes with you, not the tie you establish with Christ, but that

Christ has established with you, that he establishes with you. It is called a covenant, and God keeps his covenant. Christianity is the event of the tie that Christ has established with you. So you must say yes to this tie. Saying yes to the tie that Christ has established with you is a decision in favor of existence.

An Entreaty to God Made Man

Wolfgang Amadeus Mozart
Coronation Mass ❧ Concerto for Violin and Orchestra No. 3

Anne-Sophie Mutter
Vienna Philharmonic and Berlin Philharmonic

AGNUS DEI. With this cry, translated into the notes of his *Coronation Mass,* Mozart surely gained God's mercy: music and voice are lifted in power before the Eternal, reaching that sublime perfection which is the manifestation of the beauty he always desired.

His genius reaches this height not because he was an upright, irreprehensible person, unblemished by error; rather, he was full of contradictions and human limits, but when he created, his attachment to Jesus mysteriously made everything bright.

Thus, for me, listening to this Mass is like finding myself immersed in the freshness of early morning, when the sun is not yet completely formed on the horizon and the dawn sky announces its imminent arrival. The music moves forward like light slowly penetrating the texture of our day.

Adrienne von Speyr wrote: "Mozart at prayer has the attitude of a child, he says everything and this returns to him as melody. There is no difference between his being at the piano and his praying. The music serves to offer man an experience of prayer." The piercing insight and truth of these words were fully confirmed to me when I happened to see on television the great von Karajan conducting the *Coronation Mass* in the presence of the Pope. His conducting was a prayer, and in this he obeyed Mozart and demonstrated the great sense of responsibility that imbued his movements as he led the orchestra. I was most impressed, especially in the *Agnus Dei*, by the way the soprano followed him, the unity between the two of them. I thought to myself: each one of us is called in our lives to be an orchestra conductor—everything we encounter must carry and be a note that flows into a symphony, otherwise the things that exist would fall into nothingness.

But before the *Agnus Dei*, we hear the *Kyrie Eleison*, "Lord, have mercy," and this is the most dreadful thing that can be conceived in the life of mankind: that the creator of man might enter into humanity as a man and that men might exclude him from their lives; that the messengers of that man—who let himself be limited by the years of his life, who chose not to stretch his hand beyond those thirty-three years, except through those who have acknowledged him—may continually forget him. Forgetfulness, the lack of memory, is the fundamental betrayal. And the cry of the *Kyrie* underlines this tragedy and reminds us, who every day forget him. Forgetfulness: the forgetfulness which Christian tradition calls "sin." But God's mercy affirms itself victorious in the *Agnus Dei*. The truth of the Lord, his plan for the world, prevails for eternity. And this is peace.

Peace: this word is what marks the difference between the anguish of *Death and the Maiden* by Schubert and Mozart's *Kyrie*. They both have, as the impetus that gives them life, an experience of human powerlessness. But the human impetus, wrested from a consciousness of a destiny for which man finds himself inadequate, works in such a way that the only salvation lies in *not* thinking about it—that is the darkness that governs our lives. But this is not human; it takes away the joy of living. Immensely different is the joy that peace gives, and they find peace who live their awareness of being sinners—indeed, but sinners who are saved: *Agnus Dei qui tollis peccata mundi.* Therefore sharper, truer, much more complete is the passion which explodes in Mozart's *Mass*.

This music, to me spectacular, with that moving song, so intense and perfect, is a prayer, an entreaty raised to God made man to save the poverty and pettiness of men: this is why he came, and listening to Mozart's music gives witness to this thought.

The Divine Incarnate

Wolfgang Amadeus Mozart
Great Mass in C minor, K. 427

B. Hendricks, J. Perry, P. Schreier, B. Luxon
Berlin Philharmonic directed by Herbert von Karajan

THIS SPECTACULAR work by Mozart, which culminates in the song *Et incarnatus est* (and became flesh), is the most powerful and convincing, the simplest and greatest expression, of a man who recognizes Christ. Salvation is a presence: this is the wellspring of the joy and the wellspring of the affectivity of Mozart's catholic heart, of a heart that loved Christ.

Et incarnatus est is singing at its purest, when all man's striving melts in the original clarity, the absolute purity of the gaze that sees and recognizes. *Et incarnatus est* is both contemplation and entreaty, a stream of peace and joy welling up from the heart's wonder at being placed before the arrival of what it has been waiting for, the miracle of the fulfillment of its quest.

There came a man, a young man, who entered the world in a certain town, a certain place in the world that can be identified on a map, Nazareth. When one goes to the Holy Land, to that little town, and enters the shadowy hut where there is an inscription on the wall that reads *Verbum hic caro factum est* ("the mystery of God, here, was made flesh"), one is overcome by a shudder. This is the man Jesus of Nazareth, the chosen humanity of the word, the humanity of God—God who is the answer to the heart of man whom he created, the complete, superabundant answer to the cry of the heart he created; the cry that reverberates in the mystery of the Trinity through the presence brought about by the spirit of a Jewish man, born of a seventeen-year-old woman.

God communicated himself to man in his mortal flesh, in the time and space in which he lived—in his life as inhabiting time and space—as a lived relationship. The mystery shows himself in experience, in something we suffer, desire, mistake, do right, in something we experience: in human experience, just as it is, all of it.

Would that we too, like Mozart, could contemplate with the same simplicity and intensity the beginning in history of mercy and pardon and drink from the wellspring that is Mary's "Yes"!

This beautiful song helps us to collect ourselves in grateful silence, so that, in the heart, the flower of our "Yes" can sprout, the "Yes" by which man can act, can become a collaborator with the creator, can become even more than a collaborator with the creator, a lover of the creator. Just as it was for Mary, this girl from Nazareth, in front of the child who had come from her: a boundless relationship filled her heart and her days.

If the religious intensity of Mozart's music—a genius which is a gift of the Spirit—penetrated our heart, then our life, with all its restlessness, contradictions, all its toil, would be beautiful like his music.

An Undying Hope

Wolfgang Amadeus Mozart
Piano Concertos 20 and 24

Clara Haskil
Orchestre des Concerts Lamoureux directed by Igor Markevitch

WE STUDY WELL that music which enters as if by osmosis into one's heart; we do not really study music when we study it mechanically (do re mi fa sol la si do). What an infinite road, what a long, endless, rocky road, must 99 percent of people in the world travel to reach the tenderness of this musical way of living and, therefore, of the perception of self and of relationships of which Mozart's *Piano Concerto No. 20* is the greatest example we have in history.

Where does this feeling of self and of existence come from— so fervent, so lively, and at the same time so moved? It is quite true that man's original activity is the activity of acknowledgement and recognition. There is nothing more intense than the activity of one who, with eyes wide open, looks at a painting or a face that he likes; there is nothing more thrilling, more tense, more vibrant, in other words, more active. I think that artistic creation is no more than this; I would even say that artistic creation depends on this, it is a hard-won consequence of this, because morality is "stretching towards." "Stretching towards" means affirming a You; it is supreme gratuitousness that makes us embrace everything.

Reducing oneself to feeling a prohibition or to respecting a law without stretching to discover the hint of a greater possession is like merely sight-reading the notes. When, instead, you glimpse the second level, as in this concerto . . . it is something out of this world. You become better. Thus, though life remains dramatic, certainty and gladness, joy and peace, are the prevalent feeling that man has of himself.

Beauty is the link between the present and the eternal, so the present is the sign of the eternal, the beginning of the eternal, the initial experience of the eternal. So the taste for life begins to beat with an unmistakable note, the note of what is permanent: justice, love. In a word: the need for total satisfaction, the need for the fulfilment of the "I" (it is only thanks to a joyful presence that our heart becomes joyful in its turn: if we are alone, joy cannot spring up in us). This is the interior tension vibrating in the melody, so fascinating, so touching, so human yet so divine, because it sings of an undying hope.

Adhering to the Truth

Wolfgang Amadeus Mozart
Solemn Vespers for a Confessor, K. 339 ❧ Symphony No. 40
in G minor, K. 550

M. Pennicchi, C. Patriasz, Z. Vandersteene, J. Draijer
Netherlands Chamber Choir ❧ Orchestra of the 18th Century
directed by Frans Brüggen

THE COSMOS AND the whole of reality, of man and of human history, are like a huge building, a great work of art, a great masterpiece of God in which we are the living stones. So, it is awareness, consciousness, that opens the dimensions of being, of truth, of the beauty of the world, which is Christ—and of which the *Solemn Vespers for a Confessor*, this beautiful music of Mozart, is such an immediately absorbing and fascinating echo.

For it is wonder that makes Mozart's heart sing, and our heart along with his: wonder and gratitude before Being, which is the truth and the consistency of all things.

Starting from the senses, from the things it touches and sees, reason looks at them, penetrates them to a level that gives them a stable consistency, incomparably more dignified: eternal, participating in the truth. If it is true, it is eternal, it remains forever: *Veritas Domini manet in aeternum*. But this reason, starting from the things it knows, touching them, seeing them, and listening to them, reaches something more concrete, more stable, more consistent, more meaningful, not abstract. We say "abstract" because we do not touch it, we do not see it, we do not feel it; but what we see, feel, and hear is precisely there to lead us on to something else; otherwise, we would not know our own mother, nor our own father.

Laudate Dominum omnes gentes, laudate eum omnes populi! The beauty of this chant strengthens the heart, broadens the mind, makes the self the gathering point of waves that come from the farthest galaxies to embrace the whole world, so that everything joins together and one is forced to say, "It is," because beauty is the splendor of the truth.

Laudate Dominum omnes gentes. The Christian's goal is the glory of Christ in the world, to make Christ known in the world.

Passion for the glory of Christ, the desire that Christ be known, the desire that Christ be acknowledged, the witness to Christ: this is goal of the Christian, of the baptized, of the person chosen for this.

Laudate Dominum . . . Quoniam confirmata est super nos misericordia eius. Praise the Lord, for he has embraced us with his mercy. This is the essence of the Christian message—the mystery of God makes itself known, acknowledged, followed, loved; he educates, supports, punishes, anticipates, consoles, comforts, always placing there, on the last horizon, a strange word that man cannot understand—the word "mercy."

The Mystery is mercy: so much so that he became man, and Jesus has mercy as his supreme characteristic. The relationship between man and his destiny is mercy.

Confirmata est super nos misericordia eius. These are words that reflect the presence which is among us, with the same immediateness that causes music to give us joy. What you make me hear, what you say to me, what you call me to, what you demand of me, what you make me understand, what you call me to understand, is music. To travel in time as You want me to is music for me.

The Hand That Draws Us Out
of Nothingness

Wolfgang Amadeus Mozart
Sonatas for Piano and Violin, K. 304, 376, 378, 301

Clara Haskil, Arthur Grumiaux

WHAT EVOCATIVE power this music of Mozart has! In its initial disarming simplicity, it is like a prayer for existence!

We are radically dependent! Imagine being nothing, being nothing in this moment and emerging from nothing, with that hand that touches the nothingness and makes us emerge and that molds us, as we emerge, creating us.

There is nothing greater we can say of ourselves than this: we are "creatures." With all the fumes of our presumptions, with all the weakness of our infirm affectivity, with the inertia that makes four-fifths of our time useless, we are created. We are made, we emerge from nothingness, shaped by a hand. This hand is the fatherly hand of the Father. "Hand" is a word that understates what we are speaking of, because "hand" is a reductive metaphor; in fact, it is mystery, that hand is the Mystery. The mystery of the Father is the one who generates.

"You were and are everything for me," the poetess Ada Negri wrote. When she discovered it, at the age of sixty, she converted. "You were and are everything for me." Everything, mathematically speaking. This is what the enfolding, penetrating, persuasive music of Mozart suggests, because it is born of the experience of the

absolute gratuitous nature of the mercy of Being, which perpetu-
ally bows down over man's permanent neediness. In the tender
compassion of the heart of our God. The bowels of the earth from
which we emerge, from which we are made, the heart of the original Actor, who has molded us by his hand—*Manus tuae fecerunt
me et plasmaverunt me* ("your hands have formed me and shaped
me") (Job 10:8)—are the source of a compassion that we have for
no one, not even our father or mother! And it is only the imitation
of an Other, only the will of an Other for unity, only the love of an
Other that pours this feeling of mercy into our hearts.

What is this mercy, if not the desire, the anguished longing—in its supreme manifestation, which is Christ crucified—that
the Mystery has for our happiness? Not only for the hereafter, but
all at once, here and now! If only this mercy were to express itself
in the freshness, the precision, the powerful emotion, the mani-
fold allusions and evocations, the colossal unity, the all-embracing
unity of this sonata by Mozart! If it were possible to speak with
the voice of Mozart's music, then perhaps—or without the "perhaps"—we would be more convinced of the presence of mercy at
the root, of mercy through the whole course of life, of mercy that
takes us in its arms in the end.

The Theme of Destiny . . .
Like a Constant Background

Ludwig van Beethoven
Symphonies Nos. 2 and 7

Berlin Philharmonic directed by Herbert von Karajan

BEETHOVEN'S *SEVENTH Symphony* is like the description of a great feast. The first, third, and fourth movements are an abundant flourishing, or rather a fantastic volcano of music, of themes brimming with happiness and joy; the music would be a jumbled mess if it were not all within a profound underlying order. Imagine a huge room with guests dancing during a ball; the first movement brings us into the party, and we are struck by all the richness of feeling, color, and light that emerge from inside the hearts and bodies of the people participating in it. It seems as though everything is full of this joyous excitement.

But, at a certain point, someone, the most eccentric and bizarre of the guests, feels tired and goes outside for a breath of fresh air. He leaves the room and stops in front of a window to observe in a detached fashion all the twirling and shouting, the loud voices and music: he looks at it from outside and becomes aware of all its emptiness and vanity. Suddenly the party grows smaller and the large ballroom contracts, the people crowd together to the point that they are suffocating from perspiration and heat. The man looks with irony and sarcasm on the nothingness that, inside the room, seemed like everything; he looks with cynicism and horror on the destiny of all things. Out of this mood arises the second movement, in such apparent contradiction to the others, such that it strikes the heart with fear and trembling: the atmosphere suddenly changes. Another eye, another heart, another sensibility: another music intervenes. It is as though the music were telling the truth about what was enjoyed before.

The underlying chord is substantially always the same, one of the saddest chords ever heard in the history of music. To be sure, it contains also a very beautiful thematic melody, but the true theme is that chord, which with some slight variations lasts almost un-interruptedly from the beginning to the end; even when it seems to have disappeared, overwhelmed by the spontaneous, natural melody, man's spontaneous, natural desire to live, at the moment one least expects it, it returns to conclude the piece. This chord fills almost the entire passage and dominates it, while the melody is so evocative and rich in variations that one should be content with it, but can no longer be content with it: the theme of destiny and sadness dominates life like a background that we cannot escape.

That man is a prophet of how everything will end up in a short while, but as the second movement draws to its close, it is as though he shrugs off his melancholy mood and goes back into the ballroom to dance once again.

Like a Ray of Sunshine
through the Dark Cloud

Ludwig van Beethoven
Symphonies Nos. 5 and 6 "Pastoral"

Filarmonica della Scala directed by Riccardo Muti

BEETHOVEN'S *FIFTH Symphony* is the piece of music which, in the early days of our educational experience, taught us how to think.

Chronologically speaking, it was this work by Beethoven that I would listen to with the first students (the first ten or fifteen) who would gather together with me. I did this to re-awaken in them the ideal, risky dimension of life, without which one never does anything, becomes like everybody else, gets bored like everyone else: there is a reason why this symphony is called "the symphony of destiny." We would listen especially to the symphony's first movement, the one with "destiny knocking at the door." The beginning is the bursting in of an event. The whole drama of the orchestra develops from the event of those four initial notes that are continually repeated. In those notes is expressed the destiny that, in life, passes through the perception of bewilderment, of defeat, of sadness, and at times presents itself in its harshest aspects of trial or temptation.

Temptation is a storm, like the one described so wonderfully in the fourth movement of the Sixth Symphony, for me, Beethoven's most successful. This movement introduces, foreshadows, and describes the storm that breaks out and then passes. It passes, and everything is resolved in the sweetness of the things that are made.

But in the face of reality, there is only one way to act wherein things become an object—or rather a subject, a cause of that tenderness for which man was made: the trials we have to undergo bear witness to the way Jesus teaches, the way he renews the expansion, the explosion, the proposition of his greatness. And, in fact, devotion arouses wonder—that is, adoration—and this is the great source of prayer.

If truth communicates itself to you even through storms, then to survive the storm you must be faithful to what you belong to, and you already belong because you have recognized it as true. You would not recognize it as true now just because the sky is dark for you, but—if you are faithful—you will more easily witness something very great: the mysterious and eternal truth that reaches you like the early morning light or a ray of sunshine through the dark cloud.

The Echo of Another Beauty

Ludwig van Beethoven
Symphony No. 9 "Choral"

A. Tomowa-Sintow, A. Baltsa, P. Schreier, J. van Dam
Berlin Philharmonic directed by Herbert von Karajan

SOMETIMES, LISTENING to Beethoven's Ninth Symphony, I say to myself, "If only everything could be said with the same force of beauty with which Beethoven expresses his feelings!"

Without this perfection, how can we speak of things that are immensely more profound?

This flood of notes, that is the Ninth Symphony—this authoritative cathedral of notes that fills space with the majesty and perfection of its beauty—is nothing other than the echo of another beauty and perfection.

The notes of Beethoven's symphony are a tiny, fragile seed, a symbol of the tremendous upsurge that entered the world through a seed placed in Our Lady's womb. It is there that joy became "fact"; it is there that man's urge, his search for a destiny of happiness, receives an answer; it is there that the human intuition of a mysterious fatherhood is sustained by the certainty that everything the heart suggests has a road definitively traced out for it. And just as the seed of Beethoven's notes is majestic in the ears of his listeners, so too the seed placed in Mary's womb is irresistible. It is like an irresistible song that nothing will stop, destined to fill not only a fleeting moment of aesthetic emotion, but every expression of the human "I" and every move made in the life of the human race—that is, every expression of the history of man.

If only we could speak of certain things with the intuitive and expressive power of a genius like Beethoven! But each of us can do what he is able to do: just as our children stammer, so too do we grown-ups stammer to each other the great things for which we were made and to which we are destined. However we do intuit them a little. There is a little—approximately—of Beethoven in each of us. And for this reason, too, as we listen to the notes of this genius, our hearts are always kindled within us.

We are like a symphony, small in the face of what it should be—a bit petty, a little frightened, a little intimidated. And yet, compared to the Ninth Symphony (which, albeit in its majesty, does not last; it is destined to fade away), our cathedral, not built of notes, is made to fill history. We draw near to this destiny by obeying a task, by adhering with our freedom to the task entrusted to us. What task is this? The task of life is fatherhood and motherhood—that is, to achieve the maturity of love. The task of life is to imitate the Father by continuing the song of Jesus in history.

An Earth Planted with Truth

Ludwig van Beethoven
Symphony No. 3 "Eroica" ❧ Symphony No. 1

Berlin Philharmonic directed by Herbert von Karajan

IN HIS *DIALOGUES with Leucò*, at a certain point, Cesare Pavese makes this incandescent affirmation: "I searched for myself. One searches for nothing else." I do not know if Pavese's words fall on your hearts with the same angle of impact, but above all, first of all, on your heads, with the same angle of impact; that is, if you, too, do not feel how urgent this question is.

The sob of the second movement of Beethoven's Third Symphony is a faraway echo of a tragic affirmation of the Gospel, perhaps the only point in all the literary history of the world in which this sob—let us use the word sob—is thrown out to all mankind as a more-than-motherly warning: "What use is it if you get everything you want and then you lose yourself?"

What makes a man lose the meaning of himself, what keeps him from finding the meaning of himself? "I searched for myself. One searches for nothing else." This is the only thing a man is looking for, whatever his situation; whatever answer is given, this is what he is looking for. What stops him is violence, and the greatest violence man experiences is death.

The Third Symphony, which contains a dramatic meditation on death, sets before us the evidence that time is precarious, the fact that man is earth, dust. But to stop here, to give only this as a definition of man, would be a lie. For here is where we fight the battle with the evil one. In a contradictory and deceitful way, man opposes nothingness to Being as if he were dealing with two realities. But this is not correct, because that nothingness does not exist, since in nothingness nobody would be able to talk. Moreover, by giving in to an infantile weakness or to an arrogant lie, man unconsciously makes the mistake of identifying Being with earth, with matter, and thus, once this body is dead, Being is finished; however, this matter is made by Being, it is not self-made. The devil uses death in order to snatch man away from Being and lead him to nothingness.

In the absence of clarity in solving this last impulse of nothingness, our awareness is subjected to a limit which is denial—that is, death—and this, as a feeling, is called sadness. The mistake lies in not accepting that death is a part of life, not an objection to it. Death poses a powerful question to life: how can life be eternal? We cannot imagine how life will be beyond death; all we know is that Being will not have us lose anything of what we have here. For earth is something spectacular; without it nothing can grow. Paradoxically, earth is a precariousness seeded with something. It would not merit consideration if it were not seeded and inhabited; the earth is seeded and inhabited by truth. The earth is seeded and inhabited by the "reflection" of God's *logos*, both because of the seeds of plants and because of human seed, since Christ, the risen Lord, is the ultimate consistency of all things.

To say these things makes everything new.

The Home of the Self

Ludwig van Beethoven
Violin Concerto in D major, Op. 61 ❧ Violin Sonata No. 9 in
A major (Kreutzer)

David Oistrakh, Lev Oborin
French National Radio Orchestra directed by André Cluytens

THE TRULY ULTIMATE theme of human existence can be summed up like this: man is born *of*, he receives everything *from*. It is astonishing that nothing that belongs to our self is ours. And yet man's greatest temptation is to think he is autonomous. This temptation is so great that it coincides with the essence of original sin.

Beethoven's *Concerto for Violin and Orchestra*, which I have been listening to for fifty years (since I began teaching religion at Berchet high school in Milan), has become for me the symbol of this supreme, relentless, unending temptation on man's part to make himself the master of himself, the lord of himself, the measure of himself, despite all the evidence. Ever since the devil said to the woman: "It is not true that if you eat the apple you will die; rather, if you eat it you will become free, adult, you will be like God, you will know good and evil"—ever since then, humanity has multiplied the efforts to make itself autonomous in what pertains to culture and in what pertains to love.

But let us return to the Beethoven of almost fifty years ago. Back then, you could have seen in the streets of Milan a priest who went around carrying a huge gramophone. If someone had asked him, "Where are you going?" he would have answered, "I am going to school." "You're taking a gramophone to school?" "Well, the school won't let me use its own, so I'm bringing mine."

One of the first things I played for the students was this *Concerto for Violin and Orchestra*, with that fundamental theme running through the whole piece: the life of man, of society, is marked by the melody of the orchestra, from which the violin flees three times in an attempt at self-affirmation and three times is pulled back until it can rest and find peace, almost as though it said, "Finally!" The violin—the individual—in an effort to affirm itself is always tempted to break away in a fleeting burst, and in that attempt the instrument gives its best. Thus the most fascinating motifs of the concerto are the violin's, the individual who tries to affirm itself above everyone else. But the violin cannot last very long in this flight, and so it is a good thing that the orchestra—the community—is there to take it back in.

I shall always remember the thrill that went through the class when I played this piece by Beethoven for the first time at school: the violin expressed such a yearning feeling that it made us bend over. This yearning was so sensitive, so strong, that a girl seated in the second desk near the window onto the courtyard, burst into sobs. The class did not laugh. At the time I only said that the place of peace is where all irrational—or in any case, unfulfilled—impulses of instinctiveness are brought together again: in the community. In effect, what allows the violin to carry out these three solitary, brilliant flights, the three most peaceful moments in the concerto? The support of the community, of the orchestra, to which it can return at any moment, that takes it back, follows it, and grabs it back every time it runs away.

The violin is man who puts his hope in his temporary strength, which he always conceives as isolated, not as dictated by a shared origin and shared destiny. However one conceives it, this autonomy of the individual cannot be right, precisely because as such it has no true origin or destiny and thus cannot create history; it can bring forth a moment of emotion, but immediately after troubling the surface of the water it can do nothing, it does not have a goal.

The yearning that the basic theme of the *Concerto for Violin and Orchestra* arouses—that provoked the sudden sobs of the young girl—is the emblem of humanity's waiting for God.

Like a Dawn

Ludwig van Beethoven
Piano Sonatas

Wilhelm Backhaus

BEETHOVEN'S *FIFTH Sonata* calls to mind an episode when I was in seminary, which I always remember with heartfelt gratitude, because it reveals a friendship, a gratuitous love.

The religion class was entrusted to Monsignor Gaetano Corti, a teacher who loved me with sincere affection, even though he was twenty years older than me. He was a teacher, I an eleventh-grade student. He was truly a friend, showing a real, cordial, affectionately lively friendship.

Then when I celebrated my first Mass—which for him was a cause of personal joy—along with having to prepare my License, I was given the responsibility of the Sunday Mass and hearing confessions at a parish church in Milan. It happened to me on some Sundays to have to go down to Milan from Venegono two or three times, because I would arrange to do something together with one of the kids, but then when I arrived, that kid would not be home. But "nothing ventured, nothing gained," and "slow and steady wins the race. . . ." In that time, then, I was doing this exhausting task on Sundays, and when I got home in the evening I would be worn out. Monsignor Corti every Sunday for a whole year would wait for me at the piano, at the beautiful piano that was in the teachers' lounge. The first time, he said to me: "Listen, listen to this." It was Beethoven's Fifth Sonata, the most beautiful of the early ones.

This sonata in C minor is a melancholic piece, well suited to the tiredness—he had chosen it specifically for this—that came over me every Sunday evening. For it expresses the essence of the state of mind I felt as I came into the house: the yearning because the answer to the desire of our heart—the answer that is Christ—does not find a welcome in us, because this desire is not truly pursued by us. Melancholy, sadness, are a clear and moving signal that being born for happiness is not a phenomenon that concerns the individual person; it involves everyone's person and everyone's destiny. This sadness lies paradoxically alongside a lightness or a tenderness—as this sonata with its pacifying sweetness makes evident—or even a joy, because, in the end, there is an assurance: the assurance that the mystery of God, by rendering justice to everything, fulfilling everything, will save everything.

Monsignor Corti, with great discretion, in a sense identifying with the music, offered in this way the comfort of his sharing, full of reason, the weight of the day I had just lived. In the embrace of one's heaviness, one's fatigue, at a certain point the horizon opens up and everything takes on a lightness; toil, pain, physical suffering are not taken away, but one feels happy because he is supported, sustained, helped, loved. In the same way, in the itinerary traced out by the three movements of the sonata, the limitation of things is transfigured in the end, and already in the limitation itself we have an anticipation and a foretaste of the unlimited: almost a twilight, almost a dawn that is not yet here but is already present. Within the horizon of our ultimately still blind experience as men, there is already this vanishing point, and that of which reality is a sign enters into the sign and touches us, urges us, and says to us, "Let's go together." The true, the ultimate, with all its evocativeness, has become the companion to our leaden steps.

Since I was enthusiastic that first time, Monsignor Corti offered it to me again the next Sunday and the following Sunday, for the whole year. For a whole year this man, who was very busy with his studies, twenty years older than I, waited for me every Sunday, at 10:00 p.m. on the dot, when I arrived on the train (or on my bicycle) and played for me Beethoven's Fifth Sonata, for the whole year! But just try to think how I would go back, after the third or fourth time, how I would go back to my room, what thoughts were in my head, what kind of emotion I had, seeing this manner of acting like a friend!

A Promise Fulfilled

Ludwig van Beethoven
Triple Concerto in C major, Op. 56 ⟶ Fantasia in C minor,
Op. 80

Leipzig Gewandhaus Orchestra directed by Kurt Masur

THE YEARNING for happiness—which is the destiny and heart of man and is evoked in a sublime way in this music by Beethoven—passes by way of a journey where the destiny for which man was made is fulfilled, is experienced as fulfilled, is experienced as something that *can* be fulfilled. And indeed, this longing, which is shared by the orchestra and soloists and charges and imbues their various feelings, is ultimately appeased, becoming a joyful boldness along the way. All that is human is summed up in the word *destiny*, which is man's completion, his perfection and happiness: God, the Mystery, the Absolute, the You that completes the poverty of our "I," the omnipotence that is mercy and forgiveness. Man cannot make it on his own. But if one accepts the journey, one begins to experience happiness.

Everything bears the message of Christ's good plan for our lives. For he preceded us, he started first, he became one of us. So, fulfillment is possible, because he is present.

Thus the yearning for happiness becomes a journey, and on this journey what we desire begins to come true and to yield fruit. It is a joy that lasts, lives, and is nourished in perfect awareness of its limit—not our limit as creatures, but the limit of our heart:

God loves his creature, but man's heart does not respond with an equal amount of love. This is why we are so full of expectation, an expectation that cannot avoid an underlying trepidation—not an underlying doubtfulness, but certainly an underlying trepidation. And so, through his Spirit, he dominates our progress in this way.

In this case, the truest position—the only truly human position—is the one that is expressed as entreaty. And in effect, the second movement of this concerto is a great, profound, heartfelt entreaty—expressed by the powerful, heartrending voice of the cello—to a You present and close by, an entreaty resting totally on this presence, drawing its strength and certainty from it. Entreaty is enthusiasm's first breath. Because man, by entreating, acknowledges and accepts his destiny, acknowledges that he is loved; this is why it is the beginning of fulfillment, of perfection. And thus it comes about that the second movement erupts in the all-embracing enthusiasm and joy of living of the third movement.

It is the working of the spirit of God in the world, who acts through the mystery of the incarnation, death, and resurrection of Christ; the spirit of Christ is the soul of this fulfillment and, because of this, it is the source of this experience of being loved as a promise kept; this is the final destiny that Beethoven sees drawing near and whose fruits he intensely awaits.

Like an Impetuous Wind

Ludwig van Beethoven
Piano Sonata No. 17 in D minor, Op. 31, No. 2 "The Tempest" ❧
Piano Sonata No. 23, Op. 57 "Appassionata"

Wilhelm Kempff

BEETHOVEN'S *TEMPEST*, discreetly (because it is expressed with single notes rather than with loud phrases), is like the anticipated memory of the final tempest, which will bring the world back to its source, to its eternal judgment. A little of this impetuous wind, of this tempest that will bring Christ to reveal himself definitively to all men and to the whole world, comes in every time of trial, to make us reflect on whether or not life is something serious. The trials that inevitably come in life are tempests. They reveal the substantial position that a man takes up before a truth that strikes him and by which he acknowledges himself struck. It is a blow that he feels, on the one hand, as consistent with the desire that rekindles every morning, and, on the other hand, as something that sweeps away the cloud of objections with which falsehood obscures the sun, the sun which should illumine the whole of our life. So let the trials come, so as to reawaken us and redeem us, so as to reaffirm the truth in our life, so that we acknowledge the consistency and the meaning of reality and see things once more in their correct proportions.

Then the second movement describes well what this renewed acceptance of the truth that has been offered leads to: gratitude.

This emotion is the last frontier, full of consolation, that holds a consolation, and is the source of consolation, even in the most terrible moments of life. Like when the sky is totally covered with dark clouds, but on the horizon there is a shimmer of light that makes man breathe, makes him walk, despite the menacing tempest.

So no tempest can upset the peace and the security of someone who belongs to the truth. The tempest can rage and try to devastate, to pull things up by the roots, but then, as we said, it passes, and everything dissolves in a sweetness that makes us more serenely happy and affectionate, because we are more attached to the truth.

A Dialogue with the One
Who Made Our Heart

Ludwig van Beethoven
String Quartet No. 15 in A minor, Op. 132

Quartetto Italiano

"IT IS GOOD to give thanks to the Lord"; it is wonderful to recognize him! If we listen to Beethoven, just for a minute, we say to ourselves, "How beautiful!" The beauty of recognizing the Lord is of this nature, but deeper, like the taproot that deepens the barely-hinted appearance of the tree that is being born, much deeper and incomparably more stable: a total form instead of partial and ephemeral forms.

This *String Quartet* develops a quiet, intense, dense, heart-felt, and dramatic conversation with the Creator. Thus, in the consciousness that in this moment our person is springing from Being, this music becomes our voice in the personal and intimate dialogue with him and at the same time the perception of his reply. Our history is not something that happens of itself; it is not a coincidence, but a dialogue between him who who made our heart—and in every instant calls us to truth, to love, to beauty, to happiness—and the availability of our heart.

"In our nothingness, our hope is all in You. In you is the fullness of life," says a hymn for Lent. This music is a sign, a sign full of nostalgia and complete expectation of this goodness, of this mercy that knitted the fabric of our body in our mother's womb

and knitted the nature of all things from the womb of the cosmos
and of history.

The Cry of Incompleteness

Franz Schubert
Symphonies Nos. 3 and 8 "Unfinished"

Vienna Philharmonic directed by Carlos Kleiber

IF THE VIRGIN Mary could have listened to Schubert's *Unfinished Symphony*, what would she have felt or suffered? With what great and simple compassion would she have understood that cry from man, who is as if he did not exist, because he is incomplete and does not know where to go. How she would have let herself sweetly go to the second movement of the symphony, at every hint and openness toward a possibility that cannot depend on man but lies at the very heart of God's promise, or of the substance of the life God has given us, as suggested in the prayer that gives the theme to a liturgy: "God, our strength and our hope (substance of the changing present, reaching out towards the future) nothing that is valid and holy exists without You." Mary would have perceived the profound meaning of "valid" and "holy"; she would have maintained her usual boundless silence: "Without You nothing exists." Without You nothing exists, because that which truly exists is valid and holy. How she would have heard this prayer in herself in anticipation, this "yes," not the desperate cry that opens the Unfinished Symphony.

This is Schubert's most famous work as well as his greatest: as a piece of music it is unfinished, because the composer's death prevented its completion; but the incompleteness of life is also the true subject of the symphony.

The Ride of Eternity

Franz Schubert
String Quartet No. 14 in D minor, D. 810
"Death and the Maiden"

Amadeus Quartet

IN THE FIRST movement of Schubert's quartet, after the very brief, almost involuntary, passing hint at death, there is something like a sudden reawakening and life returns triumphant. The whole of the first movement is determined by the affirmation of life, as though death were obliterated. But death is a fact, and that fact sooner or later imposes itself; in the face of facts, one cannot daydream for ever.

The very beautiful second movement represents the theme of death and is like a sob in the literal sense of the term, a sob expressed by the biting of the strings: in the face of death we try to live with our usual caution, but the evidence of the fact is too strong, and in the second movement man seems to give in and cry.

But it is not possible: man cannot accept that the meaning of existence is negative; thus, in the third movement, there is a sort of debate between yes and no, between hope and despair. This third passage resembles the life of the human heart—a mixture, a mingling of the situations experienced in the first and second movement, like an ordeal of the heart in which the sad memory continues to dominate but is restrained and penetrated by the desire to go on living.

The last movement describes what we affirm when we say that reality is a sign. Death does not have the last word, just as the corruption of forms is not the truth of things. For here, the life that seems to end does not die but moves into the eternal, as a song of Adriana Mascagni says: "you make me walk in being." The fourth section, which I call the ride of eternity, is the description of a positive, victorious vibration, like a horse ride, riding in the great fields of heaven with all the company that now surrounds us, because the eternal is the truth of the present, and it is wonderful to imagine it on horseback. The Mystery that makes all things has conceived them with this positive clarity, with this ultimate love, because everything is destined for happiness. We must break through all limits, and then we begin to be happy on earth: "Whoever follows me will have eternal life and a hundredfold in this world," said the Jew Jesus of Nazareth. Only the thought of death can impart to the thoughts about life the thematic intensity, the melodic drama, and the positive clarity that emerge in the last movement of this masterpiece by Schubert. The debate between yes and no is resolved in the mysterious yes of the fourth and last movement. It is a mysterious yes because Schubert does not know the face of destiny, but he knows that there is, there must be . . . the great horse ride.

The Beauty You Cannot Abandon

Franz Schubert

Piano Trio No. 2, Op. 100 D. 929 ❧ Sonata for Violin and Piano
No. 2, D. 385

E. Istomin, I. Stern, L. Rose, D. Barenboim

LISTENING TO THIS extraordinary Trio by Schubert, I realized once again that the meaning, the sense of a thing, is made
possible by a gaze that is complete, more comprehensive of the
whole object that is before him. This discovery made me understand better all the figures, all the small parts, that make up the
work and thus give a full meaning to the piece.

When a great artist discovers a beautiful melody, sooner or
later he repeats it and that melody becomes like a refrain that,
repeated over and over again, determines our main memory of the
particular piece.

Schubert's Op. 100 Trio proposes the ideal journey of a man
(as if it were the journey of every man) who appears on the scene
of the world, a young person bouncing with positive drive: from
the start the music presents him bursting with energy and deter-
mination to get on in life. Then it is as if, as time passes and circumstances change, problems, uncertainties, and sufferings begin
to surface.

In the second movement, that vital drive is in a way challenged, tested, interrogated as to its energies and its hopes of fulfilment. Here emerges one of the most sadly beautiful melodies of

our musical tradition; the whole movement is built around repetitions and variations of this melody. It expresses the desire to get to the heart of things, and at the same time it has the awareness of the inadequacy of the means available: hence its agonizing sadness.

The next movement, the Scherzo, is like an attempt to make the journey while forgetting its dramatic aspect, cancelling the deep question with the superficial distraction of the world. This approach, however, is not reasonable.

Thus the way this ideal story comes to its close is moving: for in the final section it is as if the desire for fulfilment and human weakness are continually clashing with each other, eventually exhausting all their energies. And twice the question about destiny (the melancholy melody of the second movement) returns, as if to remind us of the fascinating, and at the same time dramatic, depth for which we are made. But in the last bars something extraordinary and unforeseeable happens, which transforms the theme and frees itself into a definitively positive reply: that mysterious fact makes the human journey toward fulfilment eternally possible.

When someone finds a beautiful melody, they want nothing else; this is what characterizes heaven: you will be unable to want anything else. This is happiness: being unable to desire anything else because you are fulfilled.

Only Wonder Knows

Franz Schubert
The Sonata for Arpeggione and Piano ✬ Trio 1 for Piano,
Violin, and Cello in B-flat major, Op. 99

M. Rostropovich, B. Britten, V. Ashkenazy, P. Zukerman,
L. Harrell

WHEN I LISTEN to Schubert's *Sonata for Arpeggione and Piano*,
I cannot help hoping that the progress of each man along his life
journey may reach the same perfection of expression—harmonic
and melodic—as this masterpiece possesses.

It is rare to hear a more beautiful and more fully achieved
piece of music than this composition. The music, so intensely full
and vibrant with sweetness, unfolds discreetly, making no attempt
to impress, accepting to be born out of what it is, as though obeying something other than the flow of the composer's thoughts and
feelings. And right here in this obedience, in the loving pursuit
of a deeper relationship with what is given, Schubert discovers
Mystery and approaches perfection.

Thus, the composer's path becomes a metaphor for human
experience. Each of us was made so that what God asks of our
life—life as vocation—may reach a perfection of harmony and
melody. Of what can joy be born if not this obedience? Because
harmony is an obedience; on the plane of freedom, of intelligence
and of love, harmony is an obedience. Whoever recognizes what
he was made for, whoever desires perfection for his life, asks for it,

follows it, obeys it. Indeed, what is the second movement of this sonata if not an impassioned and steadfast entreaty?

I imagine Schubert striving for beauty and perfection in what he was writing, open to the true and the beautiful. What human attitude reveals this openness, which is, as well, the only way to know truly? Above all else, wonder. Wonder is the gaze of contemplation, it is the consequence of the only way of truly embracing a fact, an event, an encounter. "Concepts create idols, only wonder knows," said Gregory of Nyssa, a great father of the early church. For it is only by embracing the true and the beautiful that our person is constructed. Personality is given by a consciousness of the goal, by a judgment about things, by the consciousness of the relationship of things with the goal, and by freedom as adherence, as an energy that makes us cling to the goal of our action. Every time we are reminded to listen to the *Arpeggione*, let us try to identify ourselves with the accomplished genius of Schubert, in the hope that, in the same way, the development of our personality may reach the perfection of expression to which it is called.

Homo Viator

Franz Schubert
Fantasy in C major, Op. 15, D. 760 "Wanderer Fantasy" ❧
Piano Sonata, D. 960

Alfred Brendel

MAN IS THAT level of nature in which nature becomes aware of itself. Man tries to become aware of what he is and of what the world is. Someone who does not reach the point of this desire, the intensity of this gaze and this feeling, of this contact with himself and with reality, is not a human being! Thus—like Schubert's *Wanderer*—he wanders back and forth, touches one point, then another, and cannot fit things together because something is missing, a factor is missing, and the addition, the subtraction, the division, the multiplication, never works out. Man's calculation on himself and on the world does not work out, is not aware of the factors at play, and therefore fails to reach a conclusion, a result.

But in this search for who he is, in this search for meaning, man needs a direction, an aim, otherwise his desire is transformed into resentment and violence.

The image of this world, in its least horrible, least evil, and least violent aspect, is that of a vagabond; not that of a traveler, but of a vagabond, whom Schubert feels and describes for twenty minutes in this beautiful piece. The *Wanderer* is a man who sets off, not on a journey (a journey has an ultimate aim), but a man who walks bewildered, and if there is something he can rejoice in, it is his disoriented spontaneity, at the mercy of who knows what. The vagabond sets off along his road, which is not a road because it has no aim, no mission, no finality and no end. This is why he is condemned to flee, first of all from himself, driven not by a desire but by a dissatisfaction that becomes a condemnation. Fleeing, fleeing, fleeing, and after three days running, like Schubert's *Wanderer*, after three days walking blindly, he finds himself in need of relationships, just like three days before. For three days, like a madman, he has seen nothing; and, after three days, when his madness abates, he finds himself once more in need of a network of relationships. Does this not describe many of our days and the life of so many people around us?

If, in the world, man's form is that of a vagabond, it means that Christ came among his own, but his own (his own!) did not acknowledge him, and those whom he called to belong to his greatness did not respond and were defeated by their own lukewarmness. Thus man, undefended, remains a slave of all that the more powerful brother creates so as to squeeze the last drop of blood from him, and a man who has no wife or children, who has no people, has nothing left to do but to go off and sing. The figure of the vagabond is that of a man without a people; whoever doesn't acknowledge that the Mystery, he who is the meaning of everything, became flesh cannot even acknowledge his brother and can never be a companion for another.

Christ came to save us vagabonds from uselessness, to give a safe path to our steps: how different is the *homo viator*, the man on a journey, as the Christian mindset understands him. He is full of sorrow and certainty—that is, he is humble; he is full of sorrow because he is quite aware of his inconsistency, of his betrayals, but through these there always moves triumphantly the evidence and the certainty of Christ's presence, the will of his presence, and his life is witness to his presence even through evil. Hoping against hope, *in spe contra spem*: the first great coordinate—the coordinate of love, in man, as he struggles on his journey towards destiny—is hope. *Spe erectus*, Saint Paul says, describing the Christian, standing *upright in hope*. Should he fall a thousand times a day, these falls are of course in him, but it as though they were not his own, less and less his own. Hoping against all appearances, standing upright in an invincible hope. Christ is the content of this invincible hope: everything is for the good, everything is for his glory.

As If on Tip-Toe

Franz Schubert
Impromptus, Op. 90 and Op. 142

Alfred Brendel

THESE SHORT compositions, like improvised thoughts or solitary meditations, are dominated by a feeling of sadness, of nostalgia. Yet in Schubert's music there is always an irreducible positivity, a trace of hope which gives form and meaning to what he is saying, a positivity more intuited and demanded by reason and the heart than the result of a peaceful possession. Schubert, communicating to us what is most intimate to him, is so serious with his own humanity and his own desire that he cannot avoid grasping the openness to the eternal that his heart suggests to him. Even if for him it is not the object of possession in the present, it remains all the same the acknowledged object of his desire and expectation. He approaches the Mystery as if on tip-toe, as if not deeming himself worthy of it.

Schubert's greatness lies precisely in this continual dialogue with the Mystery. It is a dialogue that has perhaps a concrete starting point or a particular face as its point of departure; but this is at once transformed into a You, which hovers on the infinite horizon. We are all as it were enveloped in something that penetrates us. If it were not to penetrate us, it would imprison us, as when someone embraces you—he does not suffocate you, but rather enfolds you, if the embrace penetrates you. This is how we are before the

Mystery of Being; this is how we should be before the mystery of Being, in the morning and in every moment of the day.

It is quite true that the Mystery cannot be wholly possessed; it is the object of experience, but it cannot be possessed—that is to say, measured, exhausted, embraced in its totality; but it is true all the same that it is possessed. It is an inexorable possession and, therefore, can be lived only in humility, the humility that should then reverberate between the human "I" and the human "you," person to person.

Dear friend Schubert, what is life's greatness? Life's greatness is the intensity with which the instant is lived as awareness of relationship with the infinite. And you have witnessed this to us. But the infinite is a man—Christ, a man who now sits at the right hand of the Father, that is to say, he lies at the root, where all things find their consistency. The whole value of life depends on the freedom with which man responds to the freedom with which God touches him. God touches you in an instant. The circumstances are the concrete instant in which God calls to me, in which Christ tells me "Come!" and I tell him, "Come Lord!" fill this instant.

The Note of Life

Frederic Chopin
Selections

Nikita Magaloff

IN THE LIFE of nature there is a part played that is creative of humanity: that of the genius. A genius is an eminently social charism, more acute than others, and people feel themselves expressed more by his creativity than when they express themselves. Thus we feel our sadness expressed better by Chopin's rhythms or by Leopardi's poetry than if we ourselves were to weave together notes and words on the matter. For example, we are feeling sad, you and I are both feeling sad, and we put on a record of Chopin. A third friend arrives, he too in a melancholic mood, whistling a melancholy tune he has thought up. As soon as Chopin begins our friend keeps silent, because Chopin expresses the sadness we have in common much better than that improvised tune.

I had heard Chopin's prelude *The Raindrop* very many times because my father liked it. I began to like it, too, as I got older—when I was nine or ten years old—because the main melody is easy to grasp and very pleasant. At first, the suggestive music of the main melody impressed me. But after hearing it ten, twenty, thirty times, once while I was seated in the parlor my father put that record on again. Suddenly, I realized that I had understood nothing of what *The Raindrop* really meant. For the real theme of that piece was not the music in the foreground, that immediate melody, so tender and suggestive. It was not the spontaneous listening to that piece that brought out its truth: its true meaning was something apparently monotonous, so monotonous as to be just one note that repeats itself continuously, with a few slight variations, from the beginning to the end. But when you notice this note it is as if the rest were to move aside to the margins, becoming as it were a frame to the picture: the picture itself consists only in this note that becomes a kind of fixation, and the "I," from the beginning to the end, is as it were struck continuously by this overwhelming feeling. That day I understood, without being able to put it into words—I sensed what it was all about. I said to myself, "That's how life is!" This piece of Chopin is so beautiful because it is a symbol of life.

In life, man is struck by things that arouse his tenderness, by things that attract him more spontaneously, things that he likes, that put him at ease, that suit his taste. In a word, what rules is what is instinctive, immediate, easy, captivating. And yet life lies beyond the music in the foreground: it is a single note, from the beginning to the end, from the time we are children until we are old. Just one single note! Once you have become aware of this note you never lose it again, you cannot lose it again: it remains a fixation, but a fixation that makes you wise, knowledgeable, intelligent. It is the fixation that makes a man: it is the desire for happiness.

That is the note that from the beginning to the end dominates and decides the meaning of the whole piece by Chopin, that decides from the beginning to the end what man's life is: the thirst for happiness. Whatever it is that you like, whatever attracts you, whatever you desire, makes you happy for a moment, but then it passes at once. And yet there is a note that remains intact, with a few slight mutations, but from the beginning to the end it remains profoundly intact, and, in its absolute simplicity, in its singularity, dominates the whole of life: the thirst for happiness. That is the note of life. It accompanies me like my thoughts: were I to remove it, life would lose its dignity. The creativity of colors and forms in which life expresses itself would become a bunch of fragments, with no origin, no aim, and no meaning. For those who no longer perceive this note, reality becomes a petty thing, whether family, friendship, business, lineage, state, or people.

All artists, in their most beautiful work, have the genius of recomposing and reproducing this monotony which is more beautiful than any variation. If you listen to the prelude following the note as a fixation, it is as if you find it hard to breathe, because you get a sort of overflowing feeling, so much so that as the piece draws to an end the note withdraws and the music in the foreground seems to have conquered, as if to say, "At last we've done it! At last we're free!" And then, in its newfound space it goes ahead for three or four notes. But just as you get around to thinking, "We're free," that fixation begins again and brings the piece to an end. The thirst for happiness, the destiny of happiness, can be obliterated and forgotten for a short time, but it comes back as an urge without which man cannot live: it marks the beginning and the end of the short passage that is our life.

We need to recognize that note in ourselves, because the "I" is like a piece of music made of that note, that has that note as its theme, even if the things that most affect us are the most superficial: instant pleasure, instant enjoyment, instant success, first impressions, reactivity, instinctiveness. That note continually destroys what is instinctive and prevents you from stopping along the way, from coming to a stop, because what is instinctive in love, in beauty, in your enthusiasm for work, in success, fossilizes you, turns you to stone. It is that dominant note that shatters the stones and moves the whole of reality during our lives; it moves it as water moves the pebbles in a brook, as the sea moves the sand. So all the questions man may ask, all the expectations he may have, end up in this note: the thirst for happiness.

In another of Chopin's works, the *Farewell Waltz*, it is as if in an exceptionally clear manner that note reveals its content, that is, man's destiny, according to a development and a human trajectory that is retold and realized through the form of the waltz itself.

The Creativity Which Springs from a Presence

Johannes Brahms
Sonatas for Piano and Violin, Op. 100, 78, and 108

Arthur Grumiaux, Gyorgy Sebok

BRAHMS'S *OPUS No. 100* is complete in itself, with its own face, its own meaning, like a fresco by Michelangelo. It expresses the yearning for beauty and happiness which is in man.

As I listened to it, I thought, what a profound difference there is between a musical work and a solfeggio. I believe that even people who have never studied music can understand this. (I studied it a little under Monsignor Nava, because in the seminary it was a required subject from the first to the fifth year of high school.) Solfeggio consists of a series of notes, each one struck as though it existed alone; they all stand alone, and each one is played after the other.

Conversely, in a work of music, the hundreds of notes of a long solfeggio are charged by the human heart, by human genius, and are combined in a mysterious way—no one could have foreseen it before—and what comes forth is a beautiful form, one that is gigantic in the Biblical sense of the term, a monument of art, like a "giant coming down the road." Solfeggio, instead, evokes the image of a shower of little pebbles falling down from the mountain.

Our life is, at the most, like a solfeggio, that is to say, many things, many little things united only in a temporal and logistical way, for a certain time and in a certain space, without a true connection between them, except one: the pebbles, tumbling down from the mountain, touch each other, crush each other, producing a brief impact which is meaningless.

Here is the point: each of us can live a life without meaning, a long solfeggio without any sense, or can discover that life—made up of little pebbles, each one with no apparent meaning in terms of the others, except a purely casual one—is really the dream of a heart, the ingenious image of an intelligence, the expression of a human being: a human word. Everything in the world is like a great bundle of notes, an enormous solfeggio without any meaning, and from a certain viewpoint, after a certain moment, it is painful, ever more painful.

What can we call the force that assails the world and turns it into a work of art, makes it a monument, a statue, a musical work, great music, so that "what I saw seemed to me to be the laughter of the universe" (Dante)? What is this energy? It is the spirit of a man!

All the notes which make up Brahms's sonata, all these notes are straining to be grabbed and placed in their proper place, so that the melody, a beautiful melody, can emerge. If these notes were dull, resistant, impervious to the creative light of Brahms's genius, we would not have this very beautiful "song" sung by the violin and piano, but one great long jarring sound; they would not move, the spirit would not move them. And instead, what harmony! Nothing happens by chance! Each note seems to fall naturally from the one before it, deepening its drama, and every melody allows us to take a new step; so that from the three movements of the sonata there emerges before our eyes the confident, sure song of a man who forcefully affirms the force of his life, facing all of life's trials.

Indeed, in every created thing—from stone to man, from flower to star—there is a longing for freedom, and freedom is the contribution one makes to the beauty of the world according to a mysterious plan, just as every drop of paint Michelangelo used to make his *Creation* aimed at becoming an expressed and expressive reality: expressed in that design, in that work, and expressive of that divine magnificence. Each of us is like a note, like a stone, like a drop of paint: alone, what are they? In fact, every individual tries—and tries hard—to find someone to be with. Those who seek to experience beauty feel that this experience, to be genuine, must be shared with another. Yet even this sharing is neither exhaustive nor definitive, as, at a certain point, it falters in the face of our inability to fully live the novelty hidden within the forms that beauty takes (art).

Each of us is made, has been made, as an active part, a collaborator in a design that is otherwise inconceivable to us, inconceivable to us because it is God's plan, the plan that the Father has for all of reality and which has a name.

Once, at school, a girl gave me a beautiful phrase by Brahms, in which he explains that what people call "his genius" is instead a totally gratuitous occurrence, something that is as though it appeared before me, even if it is inside me, but it is something different from me, and this is what makes me create. Our great artist friend Bill Congdon, too, emphasized this on many occasions. In any case, poetry, which is to say, creativity, comes through a presence. Otherwise it does not happen.

A Cosmic Embrace

Johannes Brahms
Symphony No. 4 in E minor, Op. 98 ❧ Tragic Overture, Op. 81

Philadelphia Orchestra directed by Riccardo Muti

THE PROPHET is a witness of beauty; he is the witness of what is so fascinating that one is forced to say: "It is." The character-istic of this evidence, of this beauty that sweeps one away, is its profound correspondence with our "I": this other outside us, this something outside us (which is the first thing evident to a child who opens his eyes and flings his heart wide open to life) has a fas-cinating, persuasive, irresistible characteristic: something outside us that corresponds to our "I."

Brahms's *Fourth Symphony* has a similar all-encompassing, cosmic, emotional, and dramatic insight, with its architecture of sounds that are like an embrace of space, an embrace opening up in ingenious ways. This is why Brahms is a prophet.

This symphony is like the thrust of reason that stretches to-ward reality, that opens wide in admiration at the entire world in its richness of organic particulars. This suggestion of a cosmic breadth, this echo and reverberation of the whole in the first movement of the symphony, however, already contains in certain points the perception of something more. But it is in the second movement that the reference to Mystery emerges suggestively from the very first beats. Brahms is forced, as it were, to admit the existence of something other that imposes itself on our attention.

Even if one refuses this as a structural dimension of the person and attempts to reduce his boundless need for meaning to what he himself can measure, if he is attentive and serious, he cannot avoid feeling the blow of reality: everything affirms a beyond. A man who is serious, who takes himself seriously and takes life seriously, cannot avoid perceiving, feeling, and thus admitting that there is something beyond what he sees and feels in action.

In this cosmic complex of circumstances (because the cosmos expresses simply the reasonableness of Mystery, the design of Mystery which is, by nature and definition, the opposite of chaos, muddle, and the completely absurd), in this blueprint that lets something beyond itself shine through, a fact happened, a fact that gave it a face.

When I gave a lecture to the Buddhist monks of Mount Koya in Japan, I tried to develop the idea of the world that was closest to the way they look at the cosmos. They see it as harmony among all things (a hair, a blade of grass, a flower petal). God, for them, can be reached through the image of the harmony of all things, so that every aspect, even the most minute—a pebble in the road—possesses something of the divine. But in the final three minutes I managed to say with simplicity: "You see, we Christians add just one thing: that this Mystery which you imagine like this (without claiming to define or to push imagination any further), this Mystery is a baby that was born to a fifteen-year-old girl. That baby is this Mystery. He is called Jesus of Nazareth and is present in our companionship every day, even to the end of the world."

Like the Grass of the Field

Johannes Brahms
German Requiem

G. Janowitz, E. Wächter, Vienna Singverein
Berlin Philharmonic directed by Herbert von Karajan

THE BIBLICAL images contained in Brahms's *Requiem* are so beautiful to reread: man is like the grass of the field that is there in the morning and in the evening has withered and died. Just as we are in the great garden of the world.

What are we before God? Not even the whole of human genius can answer this question, not even Brahms's music can answer it; rather, his music intensifies it and makes the contradiction even more dramatic. It is every person's problem. I still remember the philosophy teacher at the Berchet High School, at the end of the funeral of a Greek teacher, who had died in the classroom, in the course of a lesson. He shook his head and, atheist as he was, called out very tensely, "Ah, yes, death is the origin of all philosophies!" "Death is the origin of all philosophies!": meaning that this problem is the origin of every true thought, of every true concern, every human feeling. It is what characterizes all humanity. There is no humanity that is not characterized by this dramatic wound.

And it is the way one conceives of the relationship between today and tomorrow—that is, destiny. What is the tomorrow I may not reach? If I cannot reach tomorrow, today itself has no value. The value of today is tied to tomorrow, tomorrow to the day after tomorrow, and the line gets longer, not to lose itself on the horizon, but along the road towards the horizon on which the sun explodes again; for the sun hangs over the ultimate horizon, beyond it! Brahms's music has this wound in it, the wound of man's feeling, to which the sun does not bring the consolation of its own, faintly dawning, light, of its own significance.

Either life has a meaning or reality has no meaning. If life has a meaning, it is a You, it is an other; it is you, even if your face is totally unknown to me: Mystery. If it has no meaning, then all is dust, everything is destined to become dust, dust of the desert, or sand in the tomb of the world. This alternative is the theme of every intelligence and of every heart. Thus in his music Brahms is unable to eliminate the oppression and the heaviness that are born of the consideration of how fleeting man is. But it is a sadness and a bitterness that are only partly resigned, because in them the question vibrates: "O Mystery, how can you be everything if I am here too? I do not know."

All I do comes to dust and ashes, dust of the desert, dry and sterile; this is one of the dominant concepts of the Bible. Sterility. To be far from God is sterility; being forgotten by God is sterility. Dust of the desert or ashes of a tomb: finished. Dust and ashes. So does that mean that life makes no sense?

And yet the whole universe was brought forth for man, for this small man: "What is man that you are mindful of him?" I do not know if Brahms was able to formulate the question in this way in his heart, but his music is dramatically full of the affirmation of man's unquestionable dignity, of the perception of being made for something great.

The truth of life is not mine; the truth is that of the Mystery: "I am the way the truth and the life," that man said, the one who had said, "Without me you can do nothing."

The Mystery did not leave man alone but came discreetly to meet him. Like a seed in the ground, in the womb of a fifteen- or sixteen-year-old girl—Mary—the mystery of God, the Word made man enters into the world, God made flesh. And in the death and resurrection of Christ, the world touches its redemption and Christ's power of eternal efficacy, of irresistible victory.

Why does God give himself to man? The great and mighty magnificent God, why does he give himself to little man? "What is man that you are mindful of him?" God gives himself to man because the little man loses his head, loses his bearings, loses his way, loses himself, and ends up where all the garbage ends up, if it were not for this gracious event. God gives himself to men, he gives his power so that man might not lose himself, so that man might realize the destiny for which God himself made him: a destiny of happiness, of truth and love, which is his own love. He gave him a destiny of living with him, or familiarity with him. What a great fact: that we have been called and really are children of God. And this, as Brahms perhaps never experienced, is possible right now.

The Feast of Faith

Antonin Dvořák
Stabat Mater, Op. 58 ✦ Legends, Op. 59

E. Mathis, A. Reynolds, W. Ochman, J. Shirley-Quirk
Bavarian Radio Symphony Orchestra and English Chamber
Orchestra directed by Rafael Kubelik

IT IS IN OUR LADY that the adoration of our heart finds its
example and its form. With what intensity we discover her watch-
ing Jesus from the moment when, still an infant, he first begins to
walk, until the time he dies and when he ceases to walk on this
earth after his resurrection! Imagine the look with which Mary
gazed on him: what an infinite and boundless intensity, what a
limitless awareness! And she did not yet understand, apart from
those mysterious words from the Angel: "He shall be called Em-
manuel"; for he will save his people, he will save each one of us.

Listening to the music of Dvořák, that great Bohemian composer, we have to stir up, to cultivate and renew this whole weave
of feelings, like those which filled Mary's heart. Dvořák lost two of
his children, one dying shortly after the other; this was when his
heart woke again, and he composed the *Stabat Mater*, a marvelous
piece.

We have to follow this piece in a particular way, one that is
well known to the great artists: the mode of continuous repetition.
When a vocal, resounding formula is successful—bold and beautiful, boldly conceived, expressive—then its repetition is continued

and the phenomenon is sparked there where the word becomes more profound, where the experience becomes more human. We too repeat ourselves in this way. This would be enough to give us a rule for listening to this long piece of music: follow the repetitions: *Stabat Mater Dolorosa; Stabat Mater Dolorosa; Stabat Mater Dolorosa....*

Here I want only to note, in the different aspects of the sad initial theme, the passage in which the tension mounts at the words *Mater* and *Filius* and then where it becomes collective emotion—the whole community, the whole people, is led to cry, "May I feel like you feel, Mother! Make me feel what you feel, Mother!" *Fac ut ardeat cor meum in amando Christum Deum ut sibi complaceam.* (Make my heart burn with love for Christ, God, so that I may be pleasing to him.) Make everything in me burn! Everything up to the last hair of my head. Make everything in me burn, unworthy as I am, and yet made for singing: "I adore you, Redeemer." What freedom, what ardor of acknowledgement!

"Make my heart aware of this mysterious and real strength which makes everything thrill, which brings everything to new birth. Make my heart aware of the Mystery that gives life and that has called me, a human presence that has involved me and involves itself with me." We are asked to look because, in this gaze, that which is still distracted and restless finds its peace, its strength to develop as awareness and initiative. What makes the heart vibrate is the gaze of Christ. This is why we ask for his strength. Make me able to love you, to cling to your presence, to say "yes" to you, to obey you. Make my heart burn with love for you. The first place where this love for the Mystery blossomed as a "yes" to that human presence was that young woman, Mary of Nazareth.

Fac ut ardeat cor meum: may my whole life be inflamed. *Cor meum*: in other words, the root of life, that with which everything is to be compared so that my judgment may be true, in the love of Christ. How the world laughs at this possibility! That it may be real, not spiritualistic but real, that a man like Peter, *pater familias*, with a wife and children, should say to a man younger than himself, Jesus of Nazareth, walking with him on the lakeside, "Yes, Lord, I love you." How was this possible, if Peter had betrayed him, if he was to betray him again, if every day he strayed and would do so again? How could he say, "Yes, I love you"? "I don't know, I don't know how, but I love you more than everything else, because you are the embrace of every living thing, of everything that exists. You are the one who embraces me." For me, for me, for me!

Fac ut ardeat cor meum in amando Christum Deum ut sibi complaceam. This is the great moral law. Here begins the true moral law that is the source of morality: to be pleasing to the Mystery, pleasing to that crucified man, to the mystery of God who has become man, who was crucified for me and rose again that I might become free.

This moving reflection is provoked by every note of the *Stabat Mater*. Through freedom and the cross, we realize that even what we ourselves have suffered is redeemed, becomes a redeeming force, as it did for the great Bohemian composer, who after the death of his children was able to compose this fantastic, grandiose fresco, and as it was for Our Lady.

Fac ut ardeat cor meum is almost a monotonous repetition, but it becomes the most impressive aspect of Dvořák's music: *Fac ut ardeat cor meum:* may my whole existence, the whole of me burn. We cannot avoid this totality: wherever we are, within that embrace we cannot even fasten a button without saying: "I offer it." *In amando Christum Deum ut sibi complaceam.* So that the end goal of my time, my energy, my breathing, my being, my existence, may be His glory. This is why the *Stabat Mater* concludes with that cry that causes faith to become a feast: *Quando corpus morietur, fac ut animae donetur Paradisi gloria!* (When the flesh will die, may the soul be given the glory of Paradise.)

This masterpiece of Dvořák is not the commemoration of a death but a feast that celebrates the glory of Christ in history— because he has risen in the flesh—as St. Paul assumes and foresees when he speaks of "Christ is all and in all," thus indicating the great law of history, of time and space. For in eternity, God gets what he wants; inevitably, since eternity is made only of his will. But that Christ be everything in everyone is a word of prayer, because we are not able to respond to it with our will; it is a word of entreaty, of a resolve that, if not an entreaty, is only an illusion, because we do not have the strength!

Fac ut ardeat cor meum in amando Christum Deum ut sibi complaceam. We have to admit that this is the only affirmation possible for an eternal journey, as the aspiration and hope of man: a discovery of eternity fit for man and easy, easy for him. And at the same time terrible for man, because the whole of his freedom is at stake. Jesus is the only one who pushes man to stake all his freedom.

The Heart of a Child

Antonín Dvořák

Trio No. 4, Op. 90 "Dumky" ⚭ Trio No. 3, Op. 65

Trio from Prague: A. Střižek, J. Klika, J. Zvolanek

LISTENING TO this music by Dvořák—brief, but intense, and pure like the rare mountain air—one cannot avoid going back to being a child. Dvořák embodies the heart of a child, a heart filled with emotions and ideas, as though enacting the evangelical invitation: "I bless you, Father, because you have hidden these things from the wise and the learned and have revealed them to little children."

What is needed in order to enjoy this music is to be a little like this—in other words, to be simple of heart or poor in spirit. A poor man is one who recognizes that he does not have anything: I am not anything, you—Mystery who make all things—are. The expression of one's own poverty is called entreaty.

Thus simplicity places us in front of the truth with the entreaty that it may become true, because it so closely corresponds with our nature that there is no possibility whatsoever of interfering with it. Only the entreaty that this may happen is left, and this is simplicity, like that of a child.

But the child's wonder is not limited to observing that things exist. Those eyes and that heart are full of gratuitousness, in which the truth spills over in its immediacy. The disarming simplicity of these melodies—which unfold calmly and confidently, with affectionate tenderness, joyous enthusiasm, or rapt pensiveness—is the expression of the heart of a child, who does not have to defend anything and who expects everything, expects everything trusting in the presence of his father and his mother. And so he is glad.

The clear beauty of Dvorak's music arises from his simple obedience to the nature of things: in other words, from his giving a home to the truth: this builds the whole work. The sequence of one note after the other, mysteriously suggested and followed through in obedience, opens the treasure chest of something much greater, much more powerful.

What in the artist Dvořák is an intense, unique emotion—absolutely unique and well sanctioned at a certain level of his creative sensibility—reveals itself as a suggestion for our daily living. There is some analogy with what I learned when I was ten years old and was attending the seminary: to jump to my feet when the bell that broke up the quarter-hours and half-hours rang and marked off so intensely the time of our days, interrupting everything we were doing, whether study or play; and then to follow with loyal intensity the gesture we were making, even the smallest one—like in this piece setting down notes in order on a musical staff—cosmically great, useful, and fertile.

This should be the lightness and charm of every moment of our daily life, in its continuity hour by hour, just as it was for Dvořák: note by note, mysteriously suggested and obediently followed through.

The Beauty That Enlarges the Heart

Antonín Dvořák
Piano Quintet, Op. 81 ⋄ Piano Quintet, Op. 5

Sviatoslav Richter
Borodin Quartet

THIS MUSIC by Dvořák gives body and voice to a kind of beauty we are not accustomed to, a beauty that enlarges the heart. We are more accustomed to a kind of beauty that narrows the heart, makes it feel a lack, a nostalgia, a longing for something that is not there. Here, instead, is a deeper breath, because beauty is the door through which the Mystery presents itself to human experience and offers a glimpse of itself as the consistency of things.

During my first three years as a priest, I was at the seaside, in Finale Ligure—first in Finale and then in Varigotti, an even nicer place—and during the winter there were children in holiday camps there. I remember, as if it were yesterday, the line of children walking from Varazze to Celle, two by two on the left, because there were cars passing. In front was their teacher, a burly young lady, who was holding one of the children by the finger, a small child called Maria with curly hair. Along the road were tamarisk trees in bloom with long "hair," so, as soon as there was the slightest breeze, the tamarisks were the first things to quiver, like poplar leaves. I was behind the young lady since I wanted to tell her something, and I heard the child say, "Miss, they are praying!" So

I thought that this child had remembered my Sunday homilies at Mass; adults do not remember because they follow themselves.

Dvořák is like a child who looks at destiny with his eyes wide open; with simplicity, he entrusts himself to the Mystery who makes all things and so grasps the initiative, the suggestion of a dialogue that reality contains.

Dvořák's *Quintet* accompanies our gaze, a gaze open to how things point to what lies beyond them, to that of which they are made, for which they are made, and they draw us along like a mother and father drawing their little child along. They draw us along and lead us where we have to go—that is, to Christ, the consistency of all things. All this music is pervaded by a buoyancy which is characteristic of the simple man, who entrusts himself to the source of gladness. In this being open, in this gaze, in this loving affirmation of reality, a thrill of joy is affirmed—just a hint, not strident, but certain, concrete, and real. How much more does this thrill of joy reach its summit in a person who is conscious!

The Mystery has become present to the point of becoming visible, a tangible presence; he has come to meet us and chosen us to embrace the whole world and draw the whole world along with him. It is this awareness, this consciousness that opens up the dimensions of being and beauty; it is this awareness of being that opens up the dimensions of the truth and the beauty of the world that is Christ.

The "I" Rediscovers Itself in a People

Antonin Dvorák

Serenades, Op. 22 and Op. 44

Orpheus Chamber Orchestra

DVOŘÁK'S *SERENADES* are striking for their simplicity and immediateness and, at the same time, for their profundity. The music of Eastern Europe, unlike that of the West, has a profundity that cannot fail to carry in itself—to seek and to feel—the essence of the people. It listens to the people; it is an expression of the people; it has the people as its dimension, and it creates the amplitude of this dimension. Western music, instead, is more individualistic. For the East, the dimension of the individual's awareness has the breadth of the people—human strength and security lie in what is for everyone, for the people. It is not possible to say fully the word "I" if not in a "We," if not in a people. The whole of human entreaty—the entreaty of the individual person—is not left to a desperate solitude but is enfolded and broadened, shared in a wider ambit, which throws back its borders and accompanies it in the search for fulfilment, for an answer. Therefore artistic expression, music, and the whole of culture are the event whose subject is the person in as much as she belongs to a people, the person who expresses in herself the awareness of a people, who realizes and incarnates in herself and translates the characteristic trait of that people. And the characteristic trait of that people is the awareness they all share—the perception of the ideal for which they move, for which everything moves. What certainty and richness generate the creativity of the individual! When the "I" identifies with the life of the people, it reaches its great maturity; its maturity becomes more and more total and full the more the "I" identifies with the whole people, the more it implicates itself with the whole of its affectivity and creativity, to the point of carrying in itself the whole people.

In Dvořák's music, the wealth of the people lives again; his music, generated by a sonship that evokes gratitude, has impressed on itself the memory of a life and of a history. Thus, the unfolding of the beautiful or painful aspects of life is lived ultimately in peace—peace that comes from abandonment to the arms of destiny. All the sentiments of experience, even those most opposed to each other, are embraced and brought to rest, and therefore life becomes a feast, an experience of beauty, as these serenades, so delicate and profound, testify to us.

The Mystery, that of which everything consists and to which everything cries out (*onne cosa clama*), is evident to the heart of a person who carries this dimension of the people.

The Festiveness of Life

Nikolai Rimsky-Korsakov
Russian Easter Festival Overture ⁓ Scheherazade ⁓
Dubinushka ⁓ The Flight of the Bumblebee

Orchestre de la Suisse Romande directed by Ernest Ansermet

IF WE STIFLE the Mystery as a dimension of our relationship with people and things, all reality becomes like a game. It falls to pieces; our gaze and our hands divide life into parts that have no connection with each other.

The drama of life is in this alternative. We perceive this very well listening to the beautiful music of Rimsky-Korsakov's *Russian Easter Festival Overture*. By way of contrast, we can imagine a nightclub: a flood of sensory provocations with no thought or structure behind them, whose goal is surrender to an unstable emotion.

The alternative in life is between the response to the Mystery which we are called to give and living according to the rule of "whatever I like." The task that has been given to us is for us and, as an example, for the world—this task is *for* the world. Christ, alone, died to call the world back to the fact of the Father; thus, no matter how few we are, we are called to this task to call the world back. There is no middle ground between the task and "whatever I please."

During the night of Holy Saturday, the fact occurred that saves human existence from the confused feelings to which it seems destined and lifts it up towards a festive task—and how great Rimsky-Korsakov is as he leads us from initial uncertainty (the profoundly dramatic atmosphere that opens this piece) to the exaltation of fulfillment (the exuberant finale)!

Reality is already in the hands of the one who conquered it, who won it back to himself; all of reality is his creation, to the point that the meaning of all of reality is his person. In him everything consists. To us falls the task of showing this meaning to everyone, to declare it, because it is something that is present—like the opening motif of the *Russian Easter Festival Overture* by Rimsky-Korsakov that, taken up again and again, pervades and unifies the entire composition and gives meaning to all the fragments of melody, which are all of man's impulses.

We are not meaningless pieces; our life is not a game! What has begun in our life is a construction, like this magnificent music. It is the relationship with the Mystery, the relationship with destiny, the relationship with happiness, that makes us radically original, like a totally different world, in this world. That everything should come together in a unity without confusion, in a harmony, in a song, in a symphony—this is truly another world.

Just as in this piece by Rimsky-Korsakov, shining with light and color, everything is ordered towards a purpose, a beauty, so in our lives what gives meaning and purpose to everything, what recreates a harmony, has entered in.

It is a companionship that, above all, opens up this perspective. It is a companionship for the world, a companionship that opens up, adopting the same perspectives as Christ's, that is to say, the redemption of the world, the salvation of the world, to shout the truth to the world, to proclaim the happiness the world is waiting for, to proclaim what the world is made of, and to proclaim the world's destiny, like the musical motif, repeated and amplified, that little by little invades and determines everything. The meaning of life for all peoples, indeed, for all of reality is borne by this people.

In Belonging, Peace

Sergei Rachmaninov
Piano Concertos Nos. 2 and 3

Sviatoslav Richter, Lilya Zilberstein
Warsaw Philharmonic Orchestra directed by Stanislaw Wislocki
and Berlin Philharmonic directed by Claudio Abbado

WHEN I LISTEN to the music of Rachmaninov, so great and so immensely dramatic—like a liturgy that is a celebration of destiny—I find myself thinking: Rachmaninov expresses what I am, and what the friend who is sitting beside me is, and the friend that is sitting in front of me. For the Russian master's concertos are not outside the experience of a vitality and of a humanity lived with spontaneity: those notes, strong and dramatic, represent the heart of eating and drinking, laughing and weeping, and the tiredness that hits us and makes us fall asleep. They express the greatness of our presence in the cosmos. They give peace, too: in every movement the undaunted resistance of the positivity of things inexorably overcomes every fear that invades the mind and heart and threatens to destroy the word, the mind, and the heart, reducing everything to nothing in the "night of the world."

The night of the world is when no one thinks, when the light that enlightens from the depths of the heart to the furthest horizon of the eyes is shining in no one. The depth of the heart, though beyond our grasp, our description, and our fathoming, is the last horizon of the eyes, the content of an experience that is possible, that we are called to have, where there is an echo of the final resurrection. Every day we are called to experience this subtle and discreet impact of the resurrection, so that in the darkness of the world we keep vigil in the night, while no one is thinking and therefore is in darkness (T.S. Eliot called it "darkness over the deep," speaking of a world in which man, as awareness, is not there, or, as awareness, is shattered, broken, blocked by his incapacity). Amidst this darkness, we are a spot of light, a will to know, an impetus of gratuitous good, a passion for man's good, a passion for everyone's destiny, and therefore for our own personal destiny.

Of Rachmaninov's concertos, the most beautiful one for me, the one I like most, is the second, though there is no comparison with his other masterpiece, the *All-Night Vigil*. The second concerto is more combative and less calm than the third, though that is also very beautiful. It's like a temple of notes, of harmonies, of chords that makes us, the amazed listeners, more serene and vibrant. In this concerto can be found the whole unity of the genius of the Eastern spirit.

It is a different music from that of the West; when I think of Beethoven, for example, I cannot avoid comparing him with Rachmaninov. When I listen to Beethoven's *Concerto for Violin*, I picture the person who, in all his stature of inexhaustible desire, throws himself in a dramatic movement towards destiny, towards the infinite meaning of all things: the violin is like the individual who takes to his wings from among the rest of the orchestra. In Rachmaninov, instead, I perceive the human "I" as it is lifted up— literally made to emerge—evoked through and within a company, a chorus. The piano gives voice to this, immersing itself deeper and deeper into the notes of the whole orchestra. In Beethoven, the music expresses the "I" in its singularity; in Rachmaninov, it expresses man as part of a people, made peaceful in his belonging to a unity that exalts every single note as it fills it out. It is this peace that man searches for more than anything else, whether he is aware of it or not, in all the unquiet movements of his heart, up to the furthest horizon of his eyes.

The Hidden Harmony

Sergei Rachmaninov
All-Night Vigil

Russian State Chorus directed by Aleksandr Svešnikov

"THE HIDDEN harmony is more powerful than the manifest," says Heraclitus in a profound statement. And the *All-Night Vigil* by Rachmaninov, in which earth joins heaven's song, hide a full, certain and at the same time restrained joy—a joy that has not yet totally exploded, as though awaiting its complete manifestation. The painting by Fra Angelico comes to mind, in which Jesus is shown blocking Mary Magdalene as she tries to grab him: "*Noli me tangere*, Don't touch me, I have not yet risen into heaven, to take definitive possession of everything." But the risen one is there, present and alive. Christ, in whom everything consists, has already begun manifesting his dominion over reality. And the chorus underlines this over and over again throughout the *All-Night Vigil*, now energetically, now peacefully. Everything must be seen, perceived, acknowledged, and accepted from within this depth, from this perspective, to which all the voices seem to allude.

It is the certainty of the resurrection, the triumph of the resurrection, that sustains the entreaty and ignites the joy in the singing of the *All-Night Vigil*, which is the song of the man who has been made new: it is in the flesh of our life—in the time of our days, in the time of our existence—that this renewed face of the earth must be experienced. Only the Father knows when; only the Father knows the moment in which joy becomes miracle, the experience of the fulfilled promise, but already there is gladness, the confident hope, because the confident hope is gladness, even if joy is its final explosion.

This is the genius of Russian culture: the unity of life. And the *All-Night Vigil* is brimming with this experience of what is human in all its truth.

The truth of appearance goes beyond, spills over its borders; it makes us go down into its depths until we touch the mysterious origin of all things which appear to us, of things as they appear to us, and where the destiny of all things holds its ground, both as a motion that can be perceived and as the end where their meaning, their eternal meaning, comes into focus: what they were created for, their consistency, their subsistence. Christ's conquest of things (His eternal definitiveness) is proclaimed on the day of his ascension into heaven, which begins on Easter when this *All-Night Vigil* is sung, and becomes the content of the message which from that moment is delivered to all the world, penetrating all of history. Now he is victorious over death and, by this, over all the forces which lead to death, over all the forces of reality which do not acknowledge him as Lord.

There is a second factor, a second parameter of the new life to which this music introduces us so powerfully and suggestively, and it is the one that is said during Mass: "Send forth your Spirit so that we become one Body, one Spirit." One Body and one Spirit, that is to say: unity. The capacity for unity, for bringing about unity among men, is the sign, that is, the demonstration that the truth of the world is Christ—the sign for the world, for everyone, but also for you, the sign, the thing that persuades you. And this unity is possible, in Christ.

That Your Joy May Be Complete

Sergei Rachmaninov
The Divine Liturgy of St John Chrysostom, Op. 31

The Russian State Symphony Cappella
directed by Valery Polyansky

THIS MAGNIFICENT piece by Rachmaninov, the *Liturgy of St John Chrysostom*, strikes us every time we listen to it with an unusual beauty that rarely finds comparison in other projections or creations by man.

This beautiful music—a temple of notes, harmonies, chords that makes us more serene and vibrant—contains two extremes, which I want to recall here.

The first: one does not notice it, but for eight minutes the music sings *Gospodi pomiluj*; for eight minutes it repeats *Gospodi pomiluj*: "Lord, have mercy!" Mystery, have mercy on me! Mystery, because Mystery is the Lord. Mystery is the origin of time and its meaning, because without meaning there is no time: there is nothingness or suffocation.

Why, brother Rachmaninov, do you make us repeat, for eight minutes, "Lord, have mercy!" *Gospodi pomiluj*? Because our time has had no meaning, it has not had the meaning it could have had, it has failed to achieve that total meaning which is called destiny: it has totally "lost its memory." Destiny has not been the presence that shaped something, it has not had influence on anything; everything in us has come rather from instinctive reactions, from the indolence that has kept us from moving, from the irritation or resentment that breaks through and makes anger descend into our innermost being, creating a bitter whirlpool revealing that there is anger inside you, even if it is not proclaimed and expressed.

We have wasted time! It is the first Latin sentence that my teacher had us translate in my sixth year of school: *Perditus non redit tempus* (Wasted time never returns). How negative this sentence is! How nihilistic! It has to be destroyed so that it may not come true in this nihilistic way. And how can we destroy it? This is the object of the only entreaty to the mystery of Being, the Mystery of our origins, the Mystery that underlies the dwelling place whereby we can live, the Mystery that lays the path whereby what man lives can make sense, wherein lies the imprint of destiny: "Lord, have mercy," which means "I am at fault, I have not reciprocated, I have not responded!" *Gospodi pomiluj*. Humility is the new nature, the nature of the new man, the one born of the cross and the one who finds his substance, the structure of himself, in Easter, in Christ's resurrection. Man cannot be humble if on one hand he rejects his nothingness and on the other he does not understand and acknowledge the victory of another, the victorious presence of another. It is out of this humility that the entreaty is born and the edification of oneself and others that we all desire and seek: forgiveness, which is the great imitation of the infinite.

There is a second aspect to Rachmaninov's music, like a recurring theme. It is an *Alleluia, Alleluia, Alleluia*, uttered without forcing the voice, spoken almost without daring to speak it. Within our forgetfulness and our betrayal, there is a point when Christ's victory becomes as evident as the stars in the sky, and this is a point where we are refreshed: "Lord, I thank you. *Alleluia*." Quietly, in an undertone, however. *Alleluia, Alleluia, Alleluia*.

For whoever says with sincerity, "I am at fault," the original wellspring of his form—the form of his "temple," the original wellspring of the meaning of his life—becomes not only a promise of joy, but, in an astonishing way, a foretaste, a beginning of joy! Because "everything I have told you, I told you so that my joy may be in you and that your joy may be complete."

Generated by a Christian Civilization

Sergei Rachmaninov
Preludes Op. 3, No. 2, Ops. 23 and 32

Vladimir Ashkenazy

THERE IS SOMETHING new in the world if a man belongs.
A new society, nourished by charity, is created by a belonging: it is
a belonging that changes everything, because charity is the matrix
of culture.

Think of the difference between Chopin or Beethoven and
Rachmaninov: not so much from the point of view of power
or cunning, of Rachmaninov's genius compared with that of
Beethoven (because on that level, Beethoven could be more cunning, more subtle, and more profound), but from the point of view
of the word or the human impact , and therefore of the human
impression, of the experience one has while listening to them. The
suggestive melodies by Rachmaninov, at times tender and melancholic, at times more energetic and dramatic, express the most
varied nuances of human feeling—document, with their ultimate
calm, the profound humanity that generated them. Rachmaninov
was born in a Christian society, Beethoven was born in a schem-
ing society, cunning but impotent, indebted to Christianity in its
development but made contradictory and filled with pain and evil
by its abandoning of Christianity.

This Christian matrix, which generated Rachmaninov's consciousness, is made of concrete things, of concrete relationships,

is generated by a people. It is this belonging to a people that marks the difference between Beethoven, Chopin, and Rachmaninov. This belonging is what makes the journey towards the goal straighter and less tortuous.

What certainty and richness generate the creativity of the individual! When it identifies with the life of a people, it reaches its greatest maturity; its maturity becomes total, and the more it identifies with the whole people, the more it commits itself with the whole of its affectivity and creativity, the fuller it gets, until it carries within it the people as a whole.

A String That Sings

Heitor Villa-Lobos
Works for Solo Guitar

Piero Bonaguri

I OFTEN LISTEN to Villa-Lobos's *Prelude No. 1* and *Étude No. 11* and never tire of them. They say the same thing, though they are different—the first is more lively, while the second is more dramatic. The first piece, even in its brevity, says many things by valuing and making painful use of its own question, of repeating the theme and repeating the formula; and the second time it is not the same thing—it is much more sorrowful, it is like the confirmation of its own sadness. But then, as we have always said, it is better to be sad than desperate.

I have compared this *Prelude* to Schubert's *Death and the Maiden* because one can sense that there must be a tragedy, especially behind the first theme, quite easily recognizable from the fact that there is a string that sings. It is the painful song of the heart that, in silence, brims over, like tears that soothe the soul. Then, in the middle, in the tormented soul, comes the unexpected: the runs, the hypotheses that are made; they are short, carefree, and without repetition. But only one thing is said. The only theme is that of life; it is something alive. Apart from this, repeated, there is only death, especially in the finale. Even death is part of the definition of life; in order to understand this you have to study Schubert or Dvorak's *Stabat Mater*.

Étude *No. 11* takes up this theme again and carries it further. These two pieces, so diverse in structure, have the same thought, within two different experiences. Here the theme is made at the beginning and at the end, there is no repetition of the formula, the development is vertical; then the development of the theme deepens the soul's anguish; it penetrates into the heart of the pain and passes through it. The composition is striking, since it shows clearly the art of the guitar—there are six strings that blend together and become the mirage of a united beauty. I think the best way to listen to it is to feel what it produces in oneself, and the reverberation it produces in me and in you is the evidence and fascination of a beauty.

Art opens the way for aesthetics—that is, it is the product of aesthetics. Beauty is an other who communicates herself; in art, in the beauty of the way words and sounds are used, the person has a perception of Being that is greater than her capacity for logical reflection, because in that moment Being communicates itself synthetically as an experience of beauty. As Cardinal Ratzinger says, the Church has lost its hold because it can no longer communicate beauty to men as the way to truth.

Aesthetics is a relationship; it is a way through which the creator communicates its ethic. If you have no sensitivity, then you have no ethic. Beauty is the splendor of the truth, and truth is the splendor of the Father. Only fascination for beauty moves us, stirs us. Without aesthetics, without the shock of aesthetics, it is impossible to move towards perfection, to love perfection. Aesthetics is a shock that makes you tend in a certain direction, the same direction. It is a measure that the creator spirit gives you, as creator.

When you hear music of this kind, which is authentically beautiful, you understand that God is telling you, "Look, I exist, I really do."

PART II

Moments in the History
of the Church

With the Wide-Open Eyes of a Child

Jesu Dulcis Memoria
Gregorian Chants

Amici Cantores and Antiqua Laus
directed by Enrico De Capitani

IN THE MIDDLE Ages, when they really did know how to sing, the highest musical expression was a melody made up of "a-a-a-a" that was called *jubilus* (it is still preserved in some noble museums of the territory around Milan, but the Milanese priests no longer use it), where the whole chant is one single letter "a-a-a-a," according to a musical motif that is much more fascinating than a chant with expressed words. The finest image of reason when enthralled is that of the wide-open eyes of a child. When you really love someone you are content to be there, thinking or just looking, because any word you venture to say would diminish that splendor. When you have before you something fascinating, speaking—or trying to give explanations—leaves a bitter taste in the mouth and leaves you with a kind of anger: the more you say, the less you say.

It is not important whether you are familiar with it or not: Gregorian Chant is a charism, it is a temperamental and characteristic mode of making your own words to God profoundly aesthetic. If one is not totally distracted (or even if one is distracted, because the power of this chant has enthralled him and carried him away without him realizing it), at the end, with the Amen, there is a taste of peace that this world does not know, that no one knows, no one!

There are not many people who recite prayers as we can recite them. So when prayer becomes song—as it normally should—it attains an aesthetic tension unrivalled by any other experience.

Think, for example, of one of the most serene and victorious songs in the whole history of music: the *Pange lingua gloriosi lauream certaminis* from the Good Friday liturgy. It is a song of glory, in its sublime happiness, with its certainty, power, and glory. Glory: *Dulce lignum, dulces clavos, dulce pondus sustinet*. How can we change the world, or carry the world, if we are not permeated by these dimensions? We would be wretched, or we would be like capricious children or presumptuous adolescents, who spend their life complaining; and if, by the mercy of God, the circumstances were to be in our favor, this could attenuate our lamentation a little, but we would never be a novelty in the world; ours would not be a faith that overcomes the world, nor a justice, nor a liberation.

Faith in Christ generates a yearning in us, which is the generative aspect of Christ's faith in us. The justice of the world is faith, and faith generates hope. That the glory of Christ may come is the hope of the present, not of tomorrow, but of today, of now. Faith becomes warmth; the first warmth of faith as a judgment is that Christ overcomes the world. All these songs need to be heard in the concreteness and the existence of our life, in such a way that our heart may vibrate with an intensity and a truth that are otherwise fleeting and difficult to find.

The People That Creates History

Hildegard of Bingen
Ave Generosa

Choir of the Abbey of St. Hildegard Eibingen

A DIFFERENT WAY of living, or newness of life, consists in the fact that a man pursues his destiny in all things—pursues Christ, his destiny, in all things; once he has known him, he pursues Christ, his destiny, in all things.

Hundreds of thousands, millions of people, have lived in this way and created a new civilization. Pursuing destiny in all things: "Whether you eat or drink." Was the monastery of Cluny (I take Cluny as just one example), with the hundreds of women and men who were in it, an environment that was scarcely bearable, arid, meaningless, and uninspiring? No, for those men and women, it was the most emotionally rich foundation. When we listen to the songs of Hildegard of Bingen, we hear the words and music of a woman who was closed within four walls. If we listen carefully, we have to admit with astonishment: "If we compare our so-called civilization, with that of Hildegard, ours is barbaric!" Civilization is not the discovery of new mechanisms, especially suited for going to the Moon or to Mars, or even for pulling out the roots of your whiskers instead of just the hair itself, so that you don't have to shave again for three days. That's not civilization. Civilization is something far beyond mechanisms. When you say "I" or "you,"

you are not speaking of mechanisms. The one who owns all the mechanisms, the one we have in us, is not a mechanism.

A person who meets Christ and answers yes, and follows, penetrating into this relationship, becomes a new being; she acquires a new way of looking, of knowing, of facing reality, of doing things; she acquires a new love for everything there is. "All of you who were baptized have become one thing with Christ: there is no longer Jew nor Greek, no slave nor freeman, no man nor woman, but you are all one thing in Christ." It is this people that creates history. This is why the philosopher MacIntyre wrote:

> A crucial turning point in that earlier history occurred when men and women of good will turned aside from the task of shoring up the Roman imperium and ceased to identify the continuation of civility and moral community with the maintenance of the imperium. What they set themselves to achieve instead—often not recognizing fully what they were doing—was the construction of new forms of community within which the moral life could be sustained so that both morality and civility might survive the coming ages of barbarism and darkness (Alasdair MacIntyre, *After Virtue: A Study in Moral Theory*).

Civilization is truly civilization insofar as it exalts the person according to the totality of its factors, as it follows the person on his journey to self-acknowledgment and self-expression, and makes of society a family, a "familiar" place, a people. These days, there is no longer a people, nor home, nor family, nor person. For in the present-day mentality, feelings reduced to sentimentalism prevail over reason; or, rather, feelings prevail over the heart, so much so that the heart itself comes to be identified with feelings. So sentimentalism ends up dissolving everything—all concord, all cohesion, all organism, all organization. On the other hand, for someone who lives reason seriously, all creatures, great and small, are reflections of the eternal. Nothing is foreign to him anymore; he falls in love with reality even more than a man for a woman; and when someone falls in love with Christ, the love is as ardent as the notes of a song in which you sense that there is nothing formal in the words or in what they proclaim. It is simply love—love for him. This is the victory that overcomes the world, our faith, acknowledging this presence.

The Abbess, Hildegard of Bingen, acknowledged this with a sensitivity and an intensity that you can feel in all her songs. The place where humanity recovers its life through Christ's passion is called the Church. The Church is this place that, as the song *Ave, Generosa* says, vibrates, shines out with joy.

Like a Sudden Flash of Lightning

Venite a Laudare: Marian and Christmas Lauds
Manoli Ramírez de Arellano, Alberto De Maestri

Choir of Communion and Liberation directed by Pippo Molino

LIKE A GUST of wind that dispels the morning mist, gives things their proper outline and their true proportions, warming them with color, so these songs penetrate our hearts with the freshness of their announcement, which renews our expectation. It comes like a sudden flash of lightning, a sudden light. *Venne dal ciel messo novello* (From heaven came the bearer of tidings). Though we do not know how and cannot know when, something is certainly given us: in the undeniable suggestion of it, we can cry "Come!" The answer is given, because the entreaty is an irreversible event, because Christ answers. And Christ has answered. *Da ciel venne messo novello*: this is a fact. The song sets us before a fact with the transparent immediacy and the joyous wonder that spring from the simple acknowledgment of what is evident and therefore breaks out in a festive cry. First, the simple memory of what has happened. It is the renewal of the adhesion imposed naturally by the wonder that this presence arouses in humanity, in you.

God's answer to your entreaty fills the world; in answering your entreaty, it fills the world. It does not fill the whole world except in response to the entreaty of the single person, to your entreaty. Responding to Mary's willingness, he filled the world; in responding to my willingness, he fills the world.

It is from the sincerity of this "Come" that we understand the devotion we must have to Our Lady. Devotion to Our Lady is the most rational thing there is, after the admission that the whole truth of man lies in crying out this "Come."

Ave Donna santissima—Hail, most holy Lady: I greet you, Our Lady, you who lived this willingness, moment after moment, in that cell that was your tiny home, in your daily work, in the total solitude that was yours, in the reserve that filled that solitude; but even in the awareness full of the emotion of the event that you made possible, for which you gave your life.

Ave Donna santissima: totally in keeping with the plan of the Mystery, totally in keeping with the form of the image that the Mystery had of her from all eternity. *Ave Donna santissima*: who brought forth the Son of God in her womb.

May these beautiful songs become the voice of our heart: may they reawaken our consciousness, may they enhance the desire for what is already given, and be the adoring and filial expression of our prayer.

Everything Consists in Him

Voi ch'amate lo Criatore: Medieval Lauds

Choir of Communion and Liberation directed by Pippo Molino

FOR THE MEDIEVAL world, the permanence of Christ in history was a fact: Christ really was a presence. These Lauds are the result of a simplicity, a virtue, that accepted the evidence of the wonder that man aroused.

The wonder he aroused was like a promise: a promise of something better, stronger, truer, more loving, more compassionate, more truly alive . . . it was a promise. Human life has no dignity if it is not born of the conscious relationship with its destiny, with Christ, because Christ is the destiny of all things. The Lauds are born from this moving awareness.

Che non mi sia vietato lo tuo amore, in me non possa nulla ria indignanza (may your love not be forbidden me, nothing can rid me of this wicked indignity). Indignity is defined as "ria": wicked, guilty, because we have been granted to know the meaning of our destiny. It is by abolishing this "guilty indignity" that our life is made possible, that his love—Being's love, the meaning in which everything consists—becomes familiar to us; thus we become capable of a taste for life, of certainty, hope, affection for ourselves and for others, for things, now and in the future.

Troppo perde 'l tempo chi ben non t'ama (whoever does not love you wastes too much time), because time is the fabric on which God draws his plan, his design. I think that the will not to waste time is a factor of great importance, so it becomes the criterion for judging ourselves—whether time is important for us, not to do a lot of things, but to be. What use is it if you do everything you want but then lose yourself? But to love God is not to forget the earth; to love God is the true way to live and therefore to love the world. So much so that to love God is to love your wife or husband, friends and companions, or even strangers and enemies. To love God is to love the earth truly.

And we who love the Creator, who want to love the Creator of our personality, the Creator of our way to happiness, the Creator of the possibility of our destiny and therefore of the beauty of this world as His echo, we who want to love the Creator make the words of these songs our own. So that for us, now, listening to them becomes the renewal of the acceptance awakened naturally by the wonder that this Presence arouses in us.

Voi ch'amate lo Criatore (You who love the Creator): this medieval laud expresses Mary's gaze upon her child, already persecuted and crushed by those who led society; it is the gaze and the feeling we should have for the destiny that Christ has in our daily life, mine and yours.

So on the horizon of our souls we begin to hear Magdalene's weeping, *Magdalena degna di laudare* (Magdalene worthy of praise). She was one of the first beings to be tormented by the possible alternative that Christ offered, so overwhelmed was she by the Lord's gaze, her heart pierced, like Our Lady at the thought of the rejection that surrounded her son.

So these songs make us participants in the Event, an event that runs through the whole of history, an event that will end history, the history of mankind and the history of things. It is participation in an event and therefore in an attitude of listening, of looking that we should have, and the reflection will be none other than the echo of this listening and this looking. Because the actor in this event is only one: Christ, in whom lies the consistency of each one of us, in whom the truth of human companionship finds its realization. Let us allow ourselves to be transported by the wonder and allow ourselves to be wounded by a word or by a motif, so that our heart may be moved, lose its cruelty, and be flooded with mercy.

Convinced of the Redeemer

Rosa das Rosas: French and Spanish Songs
of the 13th-16th Centuries

Vocal and Instrumental Group Psalterium

THE WORDS and music of these songs invite us above all to open ourselves up to simplicity, to the human feeling so original and pure as to be immediately convinced of its Redeemer. Here no position of wealth, of genius, of patience, of journeying together—none of all this is as strong as this simplicity and truth.

Yet we find it hard to understand them because we are far away from an approach to what is true and original—we are far away from human originality—we find it hard to identify with the Christian attitude that produced these songs and have lost the path that lead there. We need to regain the human feeling that defines the judgment of the Christian. A person who gets up in the morning and fills his time, his space, his day, with work, his relationships with people and things, animated and determined by awareness of his destiny, of his end, of the ultimate: this is an intelligent man, full of affection—this is a real man. It is the awareness, the consciousness that opens up the dimensions of "being" and of beauty; it is the consciousness of being that opens the dimensions of the truth and beauty of the world which is Christ.

What shapes and pervades these songs is the awareness that the content of time is the glory of God. The Kingdom of God, this is the content of time. These songs were born from people who were aware of having been made to share in the glory of God already present, which gives meaning to time. So too today it is through our dedication that the Kingdom of God begins.

Conversion is to stop fixing your eyes on yourself and to start fixing your eyes on Christ, on Jesus. The whole meaning of history is this ongoing change—because this change *is* ongoing—since if the stone does not press against the keystone it falls in on itself, it falls down. The whole meaning of history is this conversion: relying on Christ instead of relying on yourself. Conversion is not a question of how consistent you are; every normal concept of morality is swept away, and the source of morality is brought to light: reaching out for Christ, looking to Christ, at him who is coming, and not at yourself.

This has two effects. The first is certitude. Someone who is reaching out for Christ is certain, since his present is already moved by him who is coming. He who is coming has already begun to come through Mary. *Salve Virgo regia* is a hymn to Our Lady, the first servant of God, the person most useful to God's plan for the world, the most useful.

The second effect of joy and the supreme flourishing of joy—of happiness and peace—is gratitude. *Gaude! Gaude!* This is the color of the air, this is the transparency of the atmosphere, the light on the horizon of that place where friendship and peace between people and things is made by God, is restored to its splendor, to its value.

Injustice and Mercy

Tomàs Luis De Victoria
Tenebrae Responsories

Choir of Communion and Liberation directed by Pippo Molino

IF YOU ARE someone who listens always and only to rock music
or the like, it takes time to understand classical music. You do not
follow it the first time. It is like when my late father would drag
me along, as a boy, to listen to polyphonic music, which he liked
very much, and I was always angry, because I could not see the
order in what seemed to be a great confusion of notes and voices—
in other words, I did not have the key. The first time I began to
understand something was when, at the age of thirteen, I heard a
choir intoning Victoria's *Caligaverunt*. After the first notes, when
the second voice came in, I got the key for understanding it. From
that time I have liked polyphony more and more. All of it.

Thus I began to feel enthralled by this music that seems—
and often is—always the same, like a continuous repetition. And
yet one never tires of it, because it reveals the horizon of the soul
and the heart, filling them with light and warmth, as Victoria's
Christian heart must have been when he wrote these *Responsories*
for Holy Week. All religious efforts try to interpret the Mystery:
the Christian method instead is to repeat the word heard. To repeat—that is, to follow. You cannot repeat a word twenty times
without being changed by it.

Victoria is a great travelling-companion given to us by God—the greatest polyphonist, as great as he was humble, and therefore less famous than others. The human voice has a power infinitely superior to that of any orchestra, and polyphony represents the expressive peak of vocal music.

Victoria's *Responsories* for Good Friday are, in our memory, the highest, the most profound, and the most suggestive point of reference in religious song.

The motets of Holy Week communicate the conscious, tender, adoring, and sorrowful emotions of what Christ is for man. The *Caligaverunt* is surely one of the most beautiful pieces: as the soul is pierced through by this sublime music, we can understand easily what we normally lack and is evident here. Here what dominates is not one's own feeling for that man who is dying, but rather that man's own sorrow, sorrow for the man who is dying. *Si est dolor similis sicut dolor meus* (if there is any sorrow like my sorrow): but these are the words of those beneath the cross, of Our Lady, of Saint John. In the forefront is placed the reality of the Man-God put to death, sorrow for Christ. This chant documents an aspect of the awareness of being sinners that is not easily found: that *si est dolor* is surely the most human cry that can be heard in music, more human and more humanly religious than all music, along with the lament that follows: *sicut dolor meus*. The thing that truly breaks through—that brings about awareness of my own sin— is Christ's sorrow, like the sorrow of a child before his mother's weeping: what dominates is the other person, not concern for your own tranquility or your need to be put at peace. There is Christ's sorrow—"look all you peoples and see if there is any sorrow like my sorrow"—and sorrow for Christ, sorrow before Christ for the way we have mistreated him.

At this point Victoria leads us into a new phase: affection that is spurned, election refused, plots hatched around him, all the more treacherous because the work of a friend, a disciple. Against him are ranged the elders of the people, those who should show maturity but, now that the time has come, prove worse than the others. The high priests, religion, the Pharisees, the intellectuals of the time: "Come, let us put poison in his bread and blot him out from the land of the living," let us uproot him from the meaning of life, we do not need him to give meaning to our life [he who is the root of everything!]; let us uproot him from the land of the living; let us get rid of him. And then there are his own who abandon him: "Were you not able to watch just one hour with me?" So the world is like a great darkness in which the source of light is death, the supreme paradox: the death of life, the death of Christ.

This hatred for Christ, as Jesus himself said in his last discourse before dying, leaves its mark on history; in this hatred, the action of the father of lies develops and takes up concrete form, day after day, by means of all the various powers, whether political, economic, or clerical: hatred for him is the necessary conclusion for every human power that will not draw its conscious, humble, and dramatic origin from obedience to that supreme power that makes all things, to the destiny of victory and glory that are properly Christ's, the justice of God. The world is submerged in falsehood, says the Bible. In the end it is violence that defines the destiny of every power: "Come let us put poison in his bread, and so we shall uproot him from the land of the living," let us not speak of him anymore. This in the end is the content of the educational method the world uses in all its expressions: let no one think of Christ anymore. Christ is a name worthy of honor if you like—you can think of him while reading about him in books—but he must be totally banished from man's life as a whole, from life in society, from the family, from the raising of children, from relationships in the workplace.

Finally, the *Responsories* bring us to the killing—the height of injustice—which he accepts out of love for us. His friends are either asleep or have become traitors; the world, the intellectuals, the religious elite, the powers, plotted together. Has the Father abandoned him, too? No. It is just that his obedience has to go all the way: "Father, into your hands I commend my spirit."

But how can the terrible and the pitiful go together; how can justice go along with mercy? How can the terrible thing we are witnessing—this injustice that we hear in Victoria's polyphony and the pity of Christ expressed on the face and in the heart of Mary—coexist? It's an injustice because "every day I was with you teaching in the temple," in the light of day, among the people; you have come to catch me through treachery at night because you are in the wrong. But in the face of such injustice and greater than this injustice, his mercy overflows all bounds; because no one could be found who would acknowledge me, "no one righteous has yet been found who would acknowledge me." Mary was the only one. But it is the same for each one of us, because there is something in us—however timid, confused, or contradictory—that acknowledges you, Jesus. We have to set free this hint of true feeling, this hint of true judgment, of nascent affection, we have to set it free. We have to leave our heart free as regards what little native justice it has before Christ. With his splendid notes, Victoria invites us to do this.

Polyphony is really a peak: and yet the search for truth, living the truth, is a music even greater than Beethoven's symphonies and the motets of Palestrina and Victoria too. This is what we are called to.

The Song That Is an Experience of Faith

O Cor Soave: The Lauds of Saint Philip Neri

Choir of Communion and Liberation directed by Pippo Molino

WHAT AN IMPACT of beauty and truth these have songs on us! What intense, living devotion they provoke in us. They move us to sincere and profound piety. Saint Philip's *pietas* is the only true popular *pietas* of the sixteenth century. St. Philip Neri was able to arouse a genuine religious spirit, and these songs are the expression of a deep and extremely simple heart.

From the origins of our history, we have been singing, and we have let ourselves be accompanied by this sensibility—which we recognized at once as an educational factor for our hearts—for the freshness, vivacity, and truth with which words and music foster imagination and self-identification and bring the figures of Christ and Our Lady alive before our eyes, reawakening our awareness, and giving voice and sound to our hearts, to our entreaty.

Song has this characteristic: it leaves nothing at a purely intellectual level. To listen to the Amen of Victoria's *Ave Maria,* or the initial impact of *Cristo al Morir Tendea* is to experience an emotion that makes words less difficult. Song favors a certain emotion that makes it easier to introduce oneself into the meaning of those words; prayer becomes easier. Singing becomes the experience of faith.

These songs give voice to the whole of the human heart, nourishing the right attitude in it. This is why they have accompanied us from the start when, at the first Mass of the movement, five minutes before the beginning, I taught *O Cor Soave*. Through these songs, Christ, the companion on our way, source of our hope, day after day destroys, fights against, the restriction in our breath, repels the attack on our capacity to breathe, to see the infinite hidden behind the face of everything we touch. When we sing *O Cor Soave*, we have compassion for what he had to go through, because it is for us that his heart was pierced!

What songs, more than these, together with the *Responsories* of Victoria, introduce us into the mystery of Holy Week, the Mystery of the Redemption?

Cristo al Morir Tendea (Christ was going to his death): we can see him with our eyes, his whole life! So I understand that sin is the absence of this "stretching towards," this tension toward the elementary imitation of the figure of Christ. Sin is the absence of this tension—not of a moral tension in the sense of desire, of inclination, even to good, to virtue. If it is not a tension towards sacrifice, then even the tension to good, to value, to virtue, becomes a lie, an illusion.

The perfection of an affection, the perfection of a work, the perfection of a prayer, the perfection of an effort, of a commitment, of whatever kind, coincides or depends on the tension to sacrifice inherent in it. Without sacrifice, there is no truth in a relationship.

May these songs, with the fascination of their beauty and truth, with the ease with which they move us, introduce our hearts firmly—educate our hearts—to be aware of his presence, to the vibrant perception of his love for us, and open us up to a response.

The Mercy of Being

Gregorio Allegri ❧ Giovanni Pierluigi da Palestrina
Miserere ❧ *Missa Papae Marcelli*

The Tallis Scholars directed by Peter Phillips

MISERERE. A PERSON can acknowledge one's own sin only in front of mercy, only within the Father's recreating embrace. Allegri's chant, in its crystalline purity and in its audacious passion, abandons itself entirely to the arms of mercy. *Miserere:* having your eyes fixed on the presence, not on your own sin. This is enough: you cannot stop at your sin even for an instant. *Miserere:* interrupting the chant—apparently interrupting the chant—but actually entering into the heart of it.

Let us imagine the experience of a child when it has done wrong: still sobbing, it throws itself into its mother's arms. It is sorry, not for the harm it has done, but out of fear of losing that presence. In the same way, you will now and again feel yourself pricked by sorrow, but what pricks you is sorrow in its true nature. The true nature of sorrow is the beginning of love. So long as beauty, or the object of love, remains only at the level of attraction, it is like a clear day when there is some mist overhead; the sun is shining, but there is a slight mist; the weather is fine, but you see a veil of mist that vanishes with sorrow, that vanishes only with sorrow. After this, you continue to watch and contemplate the truth—just like the cry continues, the sound of sorrow continues. Without sorrow, there is no truth.

Were I not to discover how sinful I am, how different from the Father, like someone who runs away, the prodigal son who runs off and throws away what the Father has given him—I often forget how the Father treats me, I forget it while I am spending the day with you—I would have no true idea of myself, and so I could not maintain the true sense of the Mystery. I would not be able to discover that it is mercy. This is the greatest and most explosive revelation—the Father who embraces everyone in salvation. The figure of Christ is the merciful Father, the mercy of Being, because Being is mercy. So you cling to him, even if you are covered in dirt.

Allegri's *Miserere* is the expression of true sorrow, the beginning of a sorrow that, in time, becomes gratitude. It is the beginning of a sorrow that develops like a seed; it is the seed of a sorrow that, as it grows into a flower, becomes gratitude; it is the flower of gratitude—thanksgiving for being loved, acknowledging and accepting that you are loved. This generates something, because if it is the acceptance of being loved, then it is to love in my turn; it is a loving response, and the memory of being loved makes me a source of action, a source of creation, of creativity. The first thing that nourishes love, whose original essence is acceptance, is sorrow for the fact that this acceptance does not permeate and determine the whole of my being.

The ideal is not to get rid of all my sins; the ideal is to look at Christ, if I really want my sin to be defeated. Otherwise it is not true that we want to take away the sin; what we really want to be able to say is, "I managed it myself." To say, "Only he is," requires the humility of a beggar.

The Greatest Amen in Music History

Giovanni Battista Pergolesi
Stabat Mater

Lucia Valentini Terrani, Margaret Marshall
London Symphony Orchestra directed by Claudio Abbado

STABAT MATER dolorosa: Pergolesi's hymn helps us to perceive the mysterious joy, the paradoxical consolation, and the vigorous certainty that challenge the things that happen. It helps us always. Truly, Pergolesi is like a brother who, walking with us, sustains our shared faith, our shared memory, and the shared loyalty to our Mother, from whom the event sets out, every moment, to enter and fill our lives.

Who felt the presence of this terrible contradiction; who felt most deeply the presence of the king, of the great Mystery? Who felt most the pain of humanity's past, present, and future rejections of him, the pain of this life which humanity spends in forgetting or refusing or denying him? Who felt this pain the most? Who felt most the Mystery of his presence? Who felt most the cross, God on the cross, if not Mary? How her eyes must have been filled with her son on the cross, against the backdrop of all things, the backdrop of her own life, her son, Christ on the cross!

Let us imagine her when she woke up in the morning, imagine how she spent her day; she believed what she believed: Mary is the point where Christ was never banished, not even one inch, one cubic millimeter, one gram. She is the point where sorrow for the world's evil has been most keenly felt. This is the reason why and the way through which she took part in God's death, Christ's death. The hate the whole world lived—and was to live—reverberated through her. The hate that killed Christ was totally absorbed into the flesh, the bones, the heart, and thoughts of this girl; the truest, greatest hate that has ever existed. We cannot have compassion for Christ or participate in our Lady's sorrow unless we risk our hearts and accept the plan the Father has for our lives. This plan entails our participation in Christ's very cross: the acceptance of sorrow and sacrifice, the contradiction of life.

A human heart cannot remain indifferent to all that happens, thanks to this event which will remain until the end of the world. He dies and rises every day until the end of the world; *Quis est homo qui non fleret*: is there anyone who would not cry? We must fix our eyes on what Our Lady lives. We would not know it, but by gazing on her we can begin to know. No matter what state our heart is in, let us pray to participate in Our Lady's feelings: "Grant that my heart may love Christ God." There is nothing that can make our hearts more human than looking on Christ in sorrow, no matter what the conditions of our life and our spirit may be.

"When our flesh dies, may the glory of paradise be given to our souls": this is why Pergolesi's *Stabat Mater*, this immense cry of pain, passionately pursued and felt, ends in the most glorious music conceivable. It finishes with the Amen.

Everything we can name—our relationships, our possessions, our joy, our desires—everything has death waiting for it; everything has a limit. Only Christ takes away this limit; only Christ saves the relationship we have with our father and mother, saves the relationship you have with the man you love, saves the relationship you have with the truth which emerges from your gaze, full of curiosity, on things, saves the life you have in you, the gusto you have in you, the love you have for yourself. He saves you in paradise, but Christ's paradise begins here, because Christ rose here. This is what the Amen means, the greatest Amen in music history, which concludes Pergolesi's *Stabat Mater*. Amen: yes. Yes to whatever you, Christ, want, because only You can remove this limit. You can remove it already now in this world. Already now, nothing is lost, nothing more in this world. This is an experience we are called to live here, not tomorrow, but here, today. He is here.

Life has a destiny: Christ died for this destiny of ours, the glory of paradise. Friendship is a companionship guided to destiny. This is the Amen we live, that we can live every day of our lives; it is already the goal, the end of our actions: our friendship. The Amen of the *Stabat Mater* is a cry of joy, of glory. It is not out of place at the heart of Good Friday, because he died in order to rise and thus be Lord of time and space and reach us. The cross is a condition placed by the Father, the Mystery. What we must verify are the consequences of obedience, that is, of faith. In faith, any cross blooms in peace, in gladness, in joy, in truth, which is the joy of our humanity. Therefore, the words of the song are also a wish: "May Christ rise in all hearts." The form this joy takes is not always the same; it differs for people in each epoch of history; it differs in the various stages, for each one of us, of God's people; the form of the glory and joy arising from the cross is not always expressed in those grandiose, fascinating monuments, built in a Christian era, which dominate the surrounding plain. This glory may also be expressed by a few natives gathered in a hut or by a small group of persecuted Christians, meeting in secret to say a prayer or celebrate Mass. Whatever the case, our hearts must take on the true form of glory and joy, a form of glory and joy which means a greater truth of reason and a greater capacity for gratuitousness in our hearts.

The Mercy that Rebuilds

Joseph Haydn
The Seven Last Words of Christ

Berlin Philharmonic directed by Riccardo Muti

Father, forgive them for they know not what they do.

ONLY GOD measures all the factors of the man who acts: for us
there is only the space of mercy. So the man Jesus, addressing the
Father, says, Father, forgive them because they do not know what
they are doing. On that infinitesimal margin of their ignorance, in
dying, he built their defense, the defense of the weakness of those
men, of the limit of those men who were killing him. This was the
occasion for which the Lord, the Father, made that act of theirs
the beginning of the mystery of the Church. Christian forgiveness
is the imitation of the luminous and calm power with which the
Father rebuilds the destiny of his creatures, surprising and assist-
ing that permanent and essential desire for good of which they are
made, and which runs through all the disasters of their hysterical,
presumptuous, and impatient self-affirmation. Thus forgiveness is
an omnipotence that rebuilds upon the last remaining ounce of
freedom: Father, forgive them for they know not what they do.
Without mercy, without forgiveness, there can be no growth, because at a certain point one begins to condemn, saying, "There is
nothing more to be done"—that is, one condemns to death. But

Being is not like a doctor. A doctor may come and say, "there is nothing more to be done," and quite rightly, because as far as he is able there is no more to be done. But for Being that is not the case: there is still something to be done!

Christ dies to free us from our evil. In the heart of human chaos , of human weakness, a cry goes up for this liberation that is humanly impossible, but possible to God: Lord, have mercy on me!

Today you will be with me in Paradise

In front of the presence of Christ, all our freedom plays out. Man cannot conceive or imagine a problem more tremendous than the original announcement that God has become man; he is here, and he is calling you: I am with you always, until the end of the world! I may be the last man of all, full of mistakes and crimes, but Christ's gaze makes me free. Think of the man whom they crucified with him, of the crimes and murders he had committed: Lord, remember me when you come into your kingdom! Today you will be with me in Paradise! He was a murderer! But at a certain moment he became aware of a presence that was different, because of which he would no longer die, before which emerged the extreme expression of the sincerity of humility: I am nothing, remember me in your kingdom. The other murderer has to cry out, get angry, and blaspheme in order not to be swept along on that simple wave of the evident difference of Christ. He had to oppose something foreign to that evident difference.

The great objection to this embrace is that Christianity does not keep the promise made, that promise that Christ has made to the murderer crucified beside him: *Mecum eris in paradiso*, and that he had prophetically defined earlier as the hundredfold. And this objection is born of another aspect of our consciousness: the fear of sacrifice. If we do not fear sacrifice, we shall experience today, in every moment, every day, a greater beauty, a greater truth in our relationships, with men and with things, as a kind of prophecy, a kind of prophecy lived in the great hope, in the great promise, with which he awaits us at the end.

Mother, behold your son

The love that Christ has for humanity is full of all its human components: sympathy, tenderness, generosity, service, emotion, with that human vibration that makes Jesus close to all and wins their hearts. This humanity appears to us from the Gospel accounts as capable of an affection that, though it is for all, is not generic; rather, in expressing a preference it opens and reveals a depth of love. Many times the evangelists stress Jesus's preference as a sign of true humanity: for the rich young man of whom Mark writes, "Then Jesus looked at him and loved him"; for Lazarus, whose sisters will say to Jesus, "Lord, he whom you love is sick." It was quite true; when Jesus came to the tomb he was moved and disturbed, and the evangelist John writes, "Jesus wept." And the Jews exclaimed, "See how he loved him!" In the same way Jesus's preference for John the evangelist was evident. During the last supper together before Jesus's death, he was lying on Jesus's breast, the same John whom Jesus looks at from the cross, entrusting his mother to him: "Jesus, then, seeing his Mother and the disciple he loved, said to his Mother, 'Woman, this is your son.' Then he said to the disciple, 'This is your Mother.' And from that moment the disciple took her with him."

My God, my God, why have you forsaken me?

He saves us because he takes upon himself all our sins. The Liturgy says, "Now the plan of the Father is fulfilled, to make of Christ the heart of the world." So it is that, "He who knew no sin God made into sin for our sake [as if the Mystery of the Father concentrated on him all the sins of the world], so that through him we should become the righteousness of God." So that we could become just before the Mystery, the Mystery treated Christ as sin, as if he was sin. For "Christ redeemed us from the curse of the law, himself becoming a curse for us, as it is written: cursed is he who hangs on a tree. Christ died, once for all, for sins, the just for the unjust, to bring us back to God; put to death in the flesh, but brought to life in the spirit."

Christ, who had no sin, was made sin for us. All the sins of men, concentrated in his heart that dies and cries out, "My God, my God, why have you forsaken me?" made him into "sin." Thus he crucified in his death the sins of all men; they are already forgiven, in the sense that now all *ascesis*—the work of purification—comes to the surface, is allowed to reveal itself in us, the force that took the place of evil in the world on the cross and made peace; comes to the surface, is allowed to reveal itself in us—today, in the day towards which we are travelling, in the action in which we are engaged—what is now possible because it is already in action: that he become the form of our life, of our thinking, of our deciding, and of our acting.

Our great crime, the sin *par excellence*, is not communicating the new humanity that has been given to us. There is no graver sin than not communicating. It is to abandon Christ, to leave him alone to cry out to the world: "My God, my God, why have you forsaken me?"

I thirst

The Mystery that makes all things has showed itself in the life of man as friend and father in a historically definitive way, the way through which Christ came. "I thirst," said Jesus. "I came to bring fire on the earth: what do I want if not for it to begin burning?" Christ makes us share in his work: the fire of which he speaks is the unleashing and the manifestation of the truth of the world: its mystery.

Thus man the sinner is made a coworker in the redemption, as the great poet Péguy says in *The Portal of the Mystery of Hope*:

*God, who is all, had something to hope, from him, from that
sinner. From that nothingness. From us. He was placed in
this condition, he placed himself in this condition of having
to hope, to wait on that miserable sinner. . . .*

*In other words it depends on us.
That the infinitely more not lack the infinitely less,
That the infinitely all not lack the infinitely nothing. . . .*

*That the perfect not lack the imperfect.
That the infinitely great not lack the infinitely small. . . .*

That the eternal not lack the perishable. . . .

It depends on us that the Creator not lack his creature.

It is finished

May our days be permeated, from the very beginning, by the
certainty of the risen Christ, by the certainty that all, truly all, is
accomplished, and that therefore life is a sharing in the cross. It is
there that all is accomplished. May the sharing in the cross be a
sure joy: the resurrection! This is our certainty, that our whole life
is permeated by this certainty, so that (in the world, not outside
the world, but in the world—therefore in trials, in disagreements,
in sorrows, in doubts, in starting again) it may be determined, ultimately, by that which the cross leads to, by that which is promised
by the cross: the resurrection.

Into your hands, Lord, I commend my spirit

From the moment when Christ was nailed to a cross and cried
out: "Father, why have you forsaken me?"—which is the most human cry of desperation that has ever been heard on earth—and
then said, "Forgive them for they know not what they do," and
finally cried out, "Into your hands I commend my spirit," from that
moment, from when that man was placed on, stretched out, and
nailed to the cross, the word sacrifice has become the center, not
of that man's life, but of the life of every human being. The destiny

of every person depends on that death. From the time that man died on the cross, the word sacrifice has become a giant word and has revealed—as when the sun rises—that the whole life of every person is made up of sacrifices, is full of the terror of sacrifice, is as it were dominated by the need to sacrifice: it is impossible to avoid sacrifice—and over everything looms the greatest conceivable sacrifice, which is death.

But there is a point in history in which sacrifice began to be interesting—in other words, to touch on man's interest, his destiny: when Christ died on the cross, so that men could be saved from death and things saved from corruption, from being reduced to so many tiny worms.

Christ's cross revealed on the one hand the dominion that sacrifice has over the life of all men and, on the other hand, that its meaning is not necessarily negative, but rather mysteriously positive: it is the condition for men to reach their destiny: "By your cross, you have redeemed the world," by your cross, Christ, you have saved the world.

Jesus on the cross, before his last breath, made his own the beginning of the psalm that offers the most complete expression of the human soul, that mysterious depth for which man binds himself, unites himself to God, because he is his creature: "Into your hands I commend myself; you redeem me, Lord, God of truth" (Ps. 31:6).

PART III

A People Sings

An Epic Search for Destiny

Russian Folk Songs: Volume I

Chorus of the State Academy of Russian Song
directed by Aleksandr Svešnikov

THE MOST IMPORTANT aspect to emphasize in these Russian folk songs is the cultural value that they both witness to and evoke, because this value is not the product of individualism, but is always an event centered on the person. What is the difference between individual and person? The person is an individual who belongs to a people, that is, to a paradigmatic piece of history, where the whole phenomenon of history takes place in miniature, in a particular place and time. A piece of history is an example of the search for a destiny; the genesis of a people is a group in search of their destiny. In fact, a people is held together by a vision of their common good, but not just any common good: what gives a people its personality is an ideal, the common good as ideal, beyond all the interests and needs to be satisfied that one might list.

Thus culture embodies and expresses the genius of a people, from its way of washing dishes to its way of raising children or making a poem: the genius of a people is the consciousness that unites everyone in the perception of an ideal that makes them move, that makes everything move according to a certain ideal perception. St. Paul already recalled this at the Areopagus in Athens (the Sorbonne of the time): the movement of all peoples is for a search for God, a sort of groping. This is a splendid category of philosophy of history, or theology of history: the movement of all peoples is defined by seeking the exhaustive meaning of their collective existence on a journey.

Precisely because of the vastness of the Russian soul, the dimension of the epic as a journey to destiny emerges in a more imposing way than in the artistic formulations of other peoples. Benedetto Croce said that when an artistic expression of man has a connection with a lyrical intuition on the total level (which is another way to define the contingent human experience aimed at infinity, therefore aimed at destiny), understanding this connection with a certain attention always generates a purity. But for this feeling of purity—confused perhaps, but still an ideal feeling—to really serve—that is, to reach the point of hurting—man must be ready for sacrifice. Without this impetus that disposes one to sacrifice—therefore to the change of something in oneself, to the breaking of a way of possessing—that ethical opening, which every feeling of beauty induces, is blocked and remains only, in the best of cases, an aestheticizing sensation. True aesthetic feeling can never be without the suggestion of a purity, as the introduction of an echo of destiny into one's own human gesture.

In this musical selection from the thousand year Eastern tradition, the people is the subject of everything, the true protagonist: listening to them, there is an evident tendency to bring out a solo voice, but always within a choir. There is, in fact, no solo song that does not claim the people: thus it happens that, when the soloist sings, the people are heard, and yet it is an individual who expresses himself. While the accent of Western singing is placed on the person, Eastern singing is all centered on the people: the solo singer is always in function of the choir, which is a characteristic of the most authentic Christian pedagogy, for which all the actions of the individual are a function of the people.

I discovered all this with emotion while listening to Russian folk songs, both the choral ones—fascinating especially for the basses, whose voices are famous throughout the world—and the solo ones. Both have extremely banal titles, such as "Around the Old Poplar" or "Around the Old Pear Tree." Let us imagine the izba with the family, the small village, the little house that has a tree next to it: the hymn to the tree, to that tree, sums up all the recollection of life, one's own history, one's parents, one's ancestors.

The Russian folk song is among the highest expressions of religiosity and the truest witness to the life of the people: the experience of an incarnate humanity, and at the same time nostalgia for something that exists, even if one cannot imagine it. The Russian soul lives according to this characteristic form of strong and dramatic melancholy—clamorously expressed or even just hinted at as a background—which makes itself felt without being clarified. The song is very sad, but intense, calm, unhesitating, since it is dictated by the power of the heart that shows itself as a need for satisfaction, as a poignant need for the happiness that will come and that has not yet come. Not so Christian song, which gives voice to the dawn of a present response and therefore vibrates with a serenity and a synthesis of much greater feelings. Russian folk song expresses the person called to faith, even if he does not know it: can we therefore say that it is the only true and completely "pre-Christian" music?

The Expectation of Something
That Is to Come

Russian Folk Songs: Volume II

Chorus of the State Academy of Russian Song
directed by Aleksandr Svešnikov

I BEGAN TO appreciate Russian folk songs many years ago, when I was first in high school. As I listened to them, I would be moved to say, "What I am studying, the deep source of all our culture, is expressed so clearly in these songs from lands so far away." The conductor of the choir in those first records that I owned was Aleksandr Svešnikov, surely the richest and best interpreter of all those I have heard. The ingenious aspect of this master is his humanity: the execution is not the product of a theoretical plan, but the stirring of a humanity before an event (whether or not he is aware); for this reason it is something new.

Russian folk songs, in my opinion, are amongst the greatest in the world because they are full of nostalgia and expectation, expressing the desire to satisfy the needs of every person. Every need we have is positive: it is the expectation of something that is to come.

The journey towards destiny is the emotional content of all the finest folk songs: even the Neapolitan songs I like so much say the same thing. There is no expression of the human feeling for life so strong as Neapolitan songs. They express the singularity of the person that begins to become aware of himself and of reality and so have as their subject the individual (in the Neapolitan songs a choir is rare); in the Russian folk songs, instead, even the soloist, when he sings, is a function of the choir.

It is difficult for us to understand the Russian songs because the kind of education we have received does not always help us perceive the nature of humanity, its ontological depth, whereas these songs are precisely the most complete expression of humanity itself: there emerges in them the natural human need for a life lived in togetherness and the consequent, obvious, trust in it. Together with the perception of the Mystery (derived from the intuition that all is given), in Russian song the experience of companionship as a journey towards destiny is found.

In these songs, then, the whole of reality is perceived as a sign that refers us back to something that is not yet perfectly defined. There is in them an underlying prayer, not explicitly spiritual, but invested with all the concreteness of human life, of a humanity that is not generic; they are like a prophecy, the expectation of the Christian announcement: "And the Word was made flesh."

The Singing That Fascinated Vladimir

Russian Folk Songs: Volume III

Chorus of the State Academy of Russian Song
directed by Aleksandr Svešnikov

RUSSIAN SONGS are the most educational thing in the world. They are educational with respect to the two factors by which we live our day: the prevalence of the dullness—the excessive weight of reality—which seems to negate desire and the alleviation of this weight in the life of the community. The turbulence of things is viewed with an intelligence, an attention, and a creativity that can hardly be imagined: this gaze is born in the Russian people from their conscious experience of the bond with their origin. This is why Russian song is the most religious there is: from the natural point of view, it is the greatest expression of man's religiosity. This is not because of a particular gift of simplicity given to the soul of the Russian people: there is something that comes even before, that keeps loneliness from arising in its soul by the nature itself of the history of this people. From another point of view, it is sought out, in that it is born of the sense of Mystery. The Russian people have this root of awe at the very origin of its being a people and of its conversion. When Prince Vladimir's ambassadors approached some Christian monks, who had allowed them to enter and be present at the celebration of the Divine Liturgy, they emerged awestruck, and on their return they said to the king: "We did not know if we were in heaven or on earth, since on earth no sight so beautiful can be seen."

All men and women have a sense of Mystery, but this perception cannot be maintained alone. The Russians, conversely, are favored by their capacity to be a people; this is why I say that Russia is religious.

For them, it is impossible for human feeling not to admit its ontological structure, whereas for us in the West there is a division—and this pathology has become normal. Their strong consciousness of being a people has enabled them to resist, despite the repeated blows inflicted on them by history: they have not accepted any other hypothesis for a real consideration of relationships than that of being a people.

Their songs were born in a people that has suffered greatly and that because of this has developed a vibrant melancholy. The West, instead (in its creative and social aspect), has cut ties with its origin; this bond is present, if at all, in pragmatic terms, not as a conscious experience. Thus the life of the individual is opposed to that of the people, and in this way forms of society are generated that, even though admitting values that are at the foundation of peace and brotherhood, do not start out from a consciousness of the Mystery and of human limitations (original sin).

Listening to Russian songs, it is impossible not to hear that humanity aspires to something other and greater and at the same time feels its shame—human shame in the sense of impotence, which is not just disproportion but a sense of sin. These songs are full of shame, yet at the same time of pain that is positive.

They sing of humanity with its frailty and its glimmer of greatness.

There is another choral expression that testifies even more fully to a humanity like this: it is Gregorian chant. Russian songs and Gregorian chant have the same root of awe, but whereas the former arouse sadness and yearning, the latter brings forth peace and serenity. Thus Gregorian chant should be lived within the same context of people (and not only on liturgical occasions) as Russian song is lived, because this is the point where the "I" and the people meet.

Melancholy

Mandulinata a Napule: Neapolitan Songs

Tito Schipa

DURING ONE of the first meetings with our friends, the monks of Mount Koya—the heads of the largest and most ancient sect of Japanese Buddhism—the conversation moved to music, and I asked them if they sang, if they liked to sing and what they liked to sing. The eldest of them was keen to say that they sang, even Italian songs. We were all curious to know which Italian songs they meant. We always sing Neapolitan songs, they said, and one of them quoted *Torna a Surriento.* Instinctively I asked, "How is it that amongst all the songs of Italy you prefer the Neapolitan ones and why particularly *Torna a Surriento?*" The leader of the monks turned to me, and with his arms opened wide, said, "Melancholy."

This is the word with which he unconsciously expressed what we call the "religious sense." We all recognize ourselves in that word; in this truth of mysterious expectation we all easily recognize ourselves. The essence of the human heart is relationship with a happiness for which we wait, whose ultimate nature and whose name is unknown to us. It is the expectation of a fulfilment to which we give a name: God. What my friends the monks of Mount Koya had grasped in Neapolitan songs is precisely nostalgia—within the pulse of life—for relationship with the infinite, which emerges in human experience as melancholy, as sadness; for the whole of life is penetrated by this word.

One day there was a party in the seminary. They were all sitting down eating, and I arrived halfway through; I was one of the youngest. "Dear Lattanzio, life is sad!" I said to a friend, "But it's better that it's sad, otherwise it would be desperate." They all began to tell me in chorus, "Bird of misfortune, Leopardi, Leopardi!" A month later, though, they were all repeating that phrase. If life were not sad, because the good we have intuited is absent, it would be desperate. In the first case, life is a thirst that goes in search, in the second case it is a beggar, like Pascoli's blind man or Schubert's wanderer. Life is sad (*tristitia est boni absentis*, sadness is the desire of an absent good: you wait for it).

Sadness is the capacity of man who aspires to the infinite. The absence of sadness is the banality of a *mens* that is almost "stupid," bereft of all thought and dignity, that denies the existence of that to which the heart aspires. The human heart, the nature of the essence of the "I," is this aspiration. God made man for the sake of goodness, for the sake of happiness, so the human heart inevitably feels this yearning for fulfillment as the soul and motor of every search, of every movement. This is the ultimate positivity of life which, in the overwhelming melancholy of the melodies, is present in Neapolitan songs.

Neapolitan songs pour over those who listen to them an intensity of tenderness and passion that Tito Schipa performs with an unheard of power in his voice, an unrivalled vigor both in its voice and in its way of feeling. We have here an affirmation of loving passion expressed and lived: so we can say that these songs introduce the mystery of Christ more than any other artistic production.

One Single Root: Human Nature

Basque Songs

Oldarra Vocal Ensemble

These Basque songs are by nature completely different from each other. Some arise from an explicit Christian religiosity, while others, apparently not religious, spring directly from the beauties of nature and of life and the hardships they bring. Some are expressions of a combative sensibility (like the man who rows far from his home), others of a simple passion. In the same way, even the tunes seem to have different origins. Yet, the whole variety of these origins has one single root, human nature. If he respects this nature, the listener (whatever his origin or personal character) will find in them fascination and satisfaction.

So Basque song is the convincing exaltation of a wealth of humanity, of a more and more evident and inexorable humanity that is religiously certain.

What these songs have in common with those of other faraway peoples is their human truth.

Song

The Most Authentic Human Expression

Claudio Chieffo
È Bella la Strada

THERE IS NO higher expression of human sentiment than music. Who is not touched by a concert of strings? How can one be insensitive to the colors of a piano sonata? It seems to be the highest thing. Yet, when I hear the human voice. . . .

Song is the most authentic of human expressions—if man is man, and he is if he belongs. A child sings if his mother is nearby. As soon as there is a movement, even a small one, he sings.

And at last there came the "Flower of Forlì": Claudio Chieffo's music took hold of us all and is still with us.

The Seed

Our Lady is the tiny origin from which everything is born. I was struck when I read of Our Lady's age in a biblical commentary: fifteen to seventeen years old. This girl, living in a remote village, set the whole world in motion! We, too, are part of this "seed"; we, too, are this seed. How great the world is, and how small we are; and yet it is through this tiny seed that the greatness of Christ penetrates time and space and history and touches human hearts. Only time makes us understand what the seed is and what it has inside. You can understand what a seed is if you have already seen its development; but the first time you see a seed you cannot know what it contains.

Ballad of the Old Man

There is a sadness that indicates a journey towards something absent that we want to reach—and there is a sadness that derives from inertia. Sadness is the affirmation of a fulfillment towards which we are travelling, whereas inertia stops us, brings us to a halt. What we call God, the ancient Greeks called Fate. All the same, whether God or Fate, rational life perceives a destiny that is a task. "He has your face, your very likeness, and that terrifies me." At a certain point, it was revealed to us that this face beyond our grasp—that from which everything flows and on which everything depends—became a man, sat down like all the rest of us. He became a man among us: he is no longer a terrible face beyond our grasp, "whom I would like to see, but it is not possible." He became visible: companion on the way, a friend—and the friendship is a companionship to destiny.

Ballad of Lost Time

What is done is done! Can there be no remedy for this sadness in the heart? Oriana Fallaci said the same thing when she spoke of the arrogance that makes it impossible to balance the books, and so we waste the present lamenting the fact. For man this would be true—what's done is done! The emptiness you carry within you that day, the injustice, the falsehood you committed yesterday, is done. So the present is the slave of what happened before. And man slides from slavery to slavery down the slope of universal black nothingness. And yet there is a presence that, whatever I might have done yesterday or the day before, or a year ago, renews me, revives me! If someone loves me and still looks at me with love today, then what I have done—the emptiness, the abyss, the remorse for my falsity—are somehow challenged; I start over again,

I get up. It is like the stirring of new life—this is the presence at work.

The New Auschwitz

Of all the songs we sing, *Auschwitz* is the most terrifying and the most true. "It's not so difficult to be like them"—man's violence to man and the inhumanity of that time go on as before, and those who were scandalized by Hitler and by Auschwitz commit the same crimes, and nobody bats an eye. The time of this violence, of this destruction, is still around us: the poison of violence and exploitation is still fermenting in our personal lives, in the relationship with your boyfriend or girlfriend, with parents, schoolmates, with all that surrounds us! How much in us tastes like the poison of violence, of exploitation! The Church calls this profound malice that remains possible in the human heart "original sin." We are immersed in a reality which, since it does not acknowledge Christ, looks upon man merely as a tool for its own plans. We have to resist this world, where they can still play the violin loudly so as not to hear the cries of the dying. I do not want to collaborate in this world! But there is only one way to do it: to approach man, whoever he is, from the nearest to the farthest, the most foreign, with a love for his destiny, a profound respect, a passion for his freedom, for his energy on the journey.

War

We have to join the fight for humanity to become truly human, to live, and to achieve happiness. It is a fight that we have to begin with ourselves, so that we do not sleep and are not so blocked by a kind of metaphysical "sinusitis" that we cannot get a word out. Saint Augustine says that man must be on his guard not to be *fugitivus cordis sui*, a fugitive from his own heart, running away from himself. The great tool that society has is that of tearing us away from ourselves, spinning us around, distracting us. "I got lost when I believed in myself." Believing in yourself means letting others do away with you. So what is the alternative? To believe in the companionship that you have sensed is serious about life. When there is a serious proposal of life—proposal of the truth is unmistakable!—you feel it; even if it does not convince you, even if it does not excite you, you feel it, you sense that it is true, at least for a fraction of a second you are struck. We have to fight our war, leaning on the presence we have sensed as true and that points the way.

Ballad of Power

This song was composed in 1967, on the eve of the student revolution. When we would sing it, the leftists would listen for a while, a little bewildered, but when we came to one of the verses, they began to beat us up: "Now, tell me, how a man can hope, a man who has everything, but does not have forgiveness?" This verse is perhaps the most human and upsetting observation of all. How can a man hope if he does not acknowledge forgiveness, which is the most dramatic and convincing aspect of the relationship the Mystery has with us? How can a man hope who does not admit forgiveness as the supreme form of relationship? But a man who does not hope, for whom the feeling of his own discomfort is prevalent, becomes slave of what the world says. And, sooner or later, the world ends up winning; it imposes its denial of the certainty of human happiness. There was nothing in the world that could have really helped us. But since "we needed someone to free us from evil," God became present, the Mystery became tangibly present, flesh of our flesh.

Song for Maria Chiara

The way the Lord shaped our face in our mother's womb, and threw us into this universal comparison, is the face of a child. Being children, first of all, is an inevitable condition for being sincere, for being ourselves. It is here that unity is reconstituted, because everything stretches towards a unity, an original, simple, recomposed, organic unity, which makes one say "I"—an "I" full of attraction, of definite, endless needs, and of responsibility. The conscious and responsible "I" has the face of a child—an original positivity before everything. And the most banal sign, the sign of this original positivity, is curiosity, an optimism that can never fail, even if it is crushed by trials. If it fails, it has no other choice than the nothingness of the self, the angry nothingness of the self, the totally discouraged nothingness of the self. This curiosity is an optimism that makes one meet the world and all things with a positivity that stretches towards fulfilment.

Do Not Be Afraid

The words most used in the Bible are "faithfulness" and "forever." You must have a reason, a support, in order not to be afraid: this is the function of our companionship. His love is never-ending because our companionship is the sign. It is made up perhaps of "fools," but it is a huge thing because it is the sign of destiny present. The encounter with a reality where the memory of destiny is alive (and this can be your companion) is fundamental; but once you have encountered it, the problem is yours, it is your person. The objections, the arguments against the companionship become strong if we are slaves of a mood of discouragement; but they are powerless if we desire our destiny.

When One Is Good

If you are open to the truth, if you desire the truth, if you are kindhearted, the more reality shows itself to you in all its concrete diversity, the more you feel driven into it, are enriched by it, you are glad of it, you never stop looking into it. The Mystery is not a wall that blocks your view but an opening which you never cease to enter.

I Am Not Worthy

It is truly a bitter fact that God has brought us up in charity and in a living awareness of what human life is, of what the end of human life is, the purpose; and yet we are so unworthy of it. With every day that passes, I wonder more and more at what God does! And God makes today because he made yesterday! So it is a new reality in the world, which has entered the world; and it is a new unity that has entered the world of the Church—so we have to add that a new reality in the Church increases, unleashes what the Church is, more lovingly and more brilliantly. "You see, I have nothing to give you," but, "if you want, take me."

The Rich Young Man

God has become our companion within a human relationship; Christianity does not exist without this, and God no longer exists without this. Because the living God is this, not the God of our thoughts, of human thoughts. In the relationship with this "pure mystery," man can do everything he thinks of and everything he wants. Man is like a voice crying out in the darkness. Everyone was groping around in the dark until the sun appeared on the horizon. One of our songs tries to meditate once more on his image as he roamed the streets of Jerusalem surrounded by the crowd. The example of the rich young man introduces us to a fundamental root of our error—a kind of stupidity or superficiality which makes us think that the road to our salvation and that of the world is entrusted to ourselves, to what we do. If this is not stupidity. . . .

The Monologue of Judas

The rich young man's attitude leads us to something more bitter and evil: the figure of Judas. One can mistake salvation with one's own activity, so that the image of justice is built upon one's personal interpretation, but one can also refuse to acknowledge—and this is the case with Judas—that justice, beauty, happiness, freedom, and salvation are something greater than us, that is with us, among us. Our salvation is in something greater to which we belong, something that is visible, tangible, and that we can follow in a human form and relationship. It is easy to say, but it is difficult to accept as a criterion, since we consider our own interpretation inevitable. "It was not for the thirty pieces of silver, but for the hope that he, on that day, aroused," that he had aroused in Judas. He did not sell him for mere attachment to money. He sold him and abandoned him because the kingdom, salvation, did not correspond to his ideas. Christ's promise was different from what he had imagined.

What liberates Christianity from the ghetto of our considerations? The community, echo of the presence of Christ, the sign, the strength, the energy of his presence.

Morning Star

In his beautiful Ave Maria—the loveliest Ave Maria and the one that most deserves to become popular—it would represent an epoch of our history—Claudio Chieffo says: "may no one leave," because if you leave, it is all over. Not if the road is long, not if you go fast or slow: if you wander off, you cut yourself off. "Mother I do not deserve to behold you," just as I am not worthy to look at Christ. "Let me bring your peace to all," to everyone, to my wife, my husband, the children in school, my colleagues at work. Let us feel, touch, see, experience that he is always walking among us. The first verse is the same as the last, so the last is really the summary of the whole method that we call "God's justice" in man's salvation. "May the tenderness of your true love protect our people on the march": tenderness is being always alert; it is longing for the ocean of peace to deepen.

The Friend

"I have a great, great Friend. . . ." It is not a nursery rhyme we are singing; they are words that perhaps are not our own, borrowed words, repeated and committed to memory, so that one day they will become fused with our hearts and become one thing. It is not, however, the imprecise, vague awareness of a child; it is the penetrating look of someone who, as an adult in the faith, acknowledges that all his greatness depends on that gesture of God's humiliation, God's bending down over us. This cannot fail to provoke a rebellion, a resistance in us. If today we are tired, worn out and bleary, and the word "friend" does not vibrate in resonance with our life, it is only because we resist a God like this. He has given me the whole world. How can he give us the whole world? He gives us the meaning of the world, because he is the meaning of the world! And, search as you will, you will find no other answer as composed, as clear and comprehensive, where nothing is left out and everything finds itself in a unity that grows with time.

The Road

The whole, great, boundless universe to which life is destined stands on one point, a chance encounter. This connection between the nature of our heart and something we have the fortune to encounter is striking. It is only in the encounter that the stale taste of our living, the narrow-mindedness of our path, is all of a sudden shaken, provoked. But we need to let ourselves be struck; we need to be paying attention. Zacchaeus's attention was mere curiosity, and yet Christ penetrated that brief fissure with his look and then with his word of invitation. The possibility of our life becoming a road, a true journey, is always imminent, it can happen in any moment, but there has to be that minimum of sensitivity, of curiosity, of attention, in order that God, he who is waiting for us, can intervene. And the journey is a question of awareness, because one could travel a hundred miles and never begin. The history of life is an awareness, because for a fossil there is no history.

Martino and the Emperor

A few years ago, singing songs like this was more emotional. The tragic memories of war were close and renewed in the tragedy of 1968 and the public disorder it brought. But if we look at the society we live in today, it, too, has a disorder—a bitter, corrupt root at its foundation. If we do not oppose it vigilantly, it is perfectly analogous to the tragedy of Nazism. One of the most tragic symptoms is that there can be wars going on every day in the world and we can still live totally sheltered from it all. There is a way we can contradict this attempted dissolution of human consistency and it is to live the ideal from day to day, in daily life. This is the first way to fight against the "power," understood in the atheistic, i.e., negative, sense of the word. This is the reflection that gave rise to "Martino and the Emperor."

Ballad of Society

Man lives through his desire for contentment, satisfaction, and happiness. That bitterness be turned into joy is the inspiration, the criterion, in everything we do: in choosing one movie theater rather than another, one companionship rather than another, or getting down to study or to work, provided the bitterness be sooner or later changed into joy. This is right. For it is what reveals, as our father Dante said, the nature of man. "Each one confusedly senses a good in which his soul can find rest," in which he can reach a total satisfaction, which he desires; and this is the basic art of living. It is like the spark that is started in an engine at every movement, and everyone strives to reach complete satisfaction and struggles for it through every hardship.

Ballad of True Love

Love is a tenderness, a force, and a freedom. But if it is a tenderness, it requires that the energy of the heart be channeled and used intelligently, with freedom, with strong will. To look at a person without thinking of his destiny, at least for a moment, is not to love him. A woman who looks at her child two or three yards away from her, while it is playing, and thinks of the destiny of that child is expressing the summit of her love as a mother. When a man loves a woman, the highest moment of his affection is when he watches her working and thinks of her destiny. Without this, it is a relationship like you have with a pen—purely instrumental—or with a dog or a cat. On the contrary, it is detachment that makes you embrace the other person in a way that otherwise would be inconceivable. For the deepest embrace is that which does not touch; if you like, it touches with the eye, which is the mirror of the soul.

The People Sings Its Freedom

Lord, where is this freedom? So many cases come to mind in which human hardship, even from the economical point of view, relationships, work, can be borne with a smiling face, if faith is what determines and moves life. Freedom is faith in Christ, not a flight from our human burdens, nor forgetfulness. Faith has a great effect on the capacity to look straight at the hardship we have to bear and to be able to embrace it and bear it joyfully. Life is a trial by definition. I wish that you may always sing the freedom that faith brings, not because it eliminates the hardship, but because it gives courage, intelligence, and strength for bearing it in a more human way and because it gives us that companionship to which we can turn in our confusion and our pain. Why was this song born among us? Because of love for the truth about humanity, which finds its expression in the people. But the people is mistreated by every power that tries to bend human nature to its own particular aim, whether it be immediate or ideological, practical or theoretical.

Acknowledgments

The editors would like to acknowledge the work of those who did the initial translation parts of this book when they were first printed as liner notes for compact discs:

Ann-Katerine Grindle
Richard Sadleir
Susan Scott
Patrick Stevenson
Fiachra Stockman
Sofia Jennifer Teodori
Chris Vath

Special thanks also to Sandro Chierici, Laura Ferrario, Fr. Matthew Henry, and Angelo Sala for their assistance as we prepared this book for publication.

This book was set in Adobe Caslon Pro, designed by Carol Twombly and released in 1990. The typeface is named after the British typefounder William Caslon (1692–1766) and grew out of Twombly's study of Caslon's specimen sheets produced between 1734 and 1770. Though Caslon began his career making "exotic" typefaces—Hebrew, Arabic, and Coptic—his Roman typeface became the standard for text printed in English for most of the eighteenth century, including the Declaration of Independence.

This book was designed by Shannon Carter, Ian Creeger, and Gregory Wolfe. It was published in hardcover, paperback, and electronic formats by Slant Books, Seattle, Washington.

Cover photograph by Raymond Petrik via Unsplash.

www.ingramcontent.com/pod-product-compliance
Lightning Source LLC
La Vergne TN
LVHW090746300125
802499LV00017B/80/J